The Forward book of poetry
2009

ABOUT FORWARD

The Forward book of poetry is our way of acknowledging our indebtedness to language. After all, this is the very heartland of Forward's business: it is skilful use of language that enables us to form a connection between readers and the brand communications we create.

This is why we made a decision sixteen years ago that our contribution would be to sponsor an annual series of poetry collections to be published to coincide with National Poetry Day.

In a digital world, where the flood of sound bites is in danger of drowning more considered thought and ideas, poetry is just about holding its own against the incoming tide of ephemera. We recognise that poetry is a cornerstone of society's legacy to future generations, and by taking on the role of conservator, we can share responsibility for its preservation. It is the most sophisticated and precise distillation of language that we have; an art that demands great skill from the writer to evoke a response from the reader.

We are proud to champion a literary tradition so compelling and engaging, and play our part in creating a body of work that moves people deeply.

The Forward book of poetry
2009

LONDON

First published in Great Britain by
Forward Ltd · 84–86 Regent Street · London W1B 5DD
in association with
Faber and Faber · 3 Queen Square · London WC1N 3AU

ISBN 978 0 571 24396 9 (paperback)

Compilation copyright © Forward Ltd 2008
Foreword copyright © Frieda Hughes

A CIP catalogue reference for this book
is available at the British Library.

FSC
Mixed Sources
Product group from well-managed
forests and other controlled sources
Cert no. SGS-COC-2953
www.fsc.org
© 1996 Forest Stewardship Council

Reprographics by AltaImage
Printed by CPI Antony Rowe
Bumper's Farm · Chippenham · Wiltshire SN14 6LH · UK

To Nick

Contents

Preface

ONE OF THE MAIN IMPULSES behind the launch of the first Forward Poetry Prizes in 1992 was to try, in a small but practical way, to stimulate a wider interest in contemporary poetry. In those dim and distant days, poetry still had the unenviable – and quite unfair – reputation of being somehow rather difficult, exclusive and inaccessible. How times have changed.

The phenomenal growth of interest in poetry of all kinds since then has been one of the most rewarding aspects of running the Forward Prizes. It's a renaissance with many different manifestations, but what is particularly striking is how many more outlets there are for poetry today, a fact reflected in the wide range of sources from which we received submissions: from competitions such as the Bridport and Wigtown and a variety of poetry magazines as well as from book publishers. Entry numbers are rising too – a satisfyingly healthy 133 collections submitted this year – and I can think of few better indicators of the rude health of contemporary poetry than these.

As always, my first thanks must go to our team of judges – this year led by Frieda Hughes, superbly assisted by Fleur Adcock, Alan Brownjohn, Lemn Sissay and Natalie Whittle – who had the difficult job of choosing the finest poems from a particularly strong selection.

But there would be no Forward Prizes without our partners' continuing commitment: Felix Dennis, inimitable as always; Jules Mann and The Poetry Society; John Hampson and Arts Council England; Faber and Faber; the Colman Getty team, including Dotti Irving, Liz Sich, Kate Wright-Morris and Truda Spruyt; and, of course, everyone at Forward, without whom this whole wonderful journey would never have begun.

William Sieghart

Foreword

EACH POET HAS THEIR OWN LANGUAGE and store of imagery, which continues to evolve throughout their lives. Reading the wealth of publications submitted for the Forward Prizes from cover to cover has provided a fascinating overview of this evolution: new and emerging poets bring us their fresh voices and startling visions and in our minds we begin to chart their journey, while poets whose work is already familiar bring their insight and experience, adding further chapters to their individual odysseys.

Impressions of each poet and the world that they inhabit arise from the pages, creating a presence in our heads born of our reaction to submersion in their work. We absorb their likes and dislikes, their obsessions and preoccupations, and the ways in which they reflect what affects them. In reading a poetry collection right through, even the order of the poems that each poet chooses for his or her book can affect us, since the mind cannot help but be influenced by what just happened – or was read – a moment ago.

Because of the sheer number of books, markers – or signposts – born of a significant image or idea became more notable than, perhaps, if one had been reading only a single volume. Jen Hadfield's 'Canis Minor' in *Nigh-No-Place* describes a dog that waits 'like a little headstone', and I can see its bony cranium resting in the dirt; the phrase (and title) in one of Catherine Smith's poems from her book *Lip* – 'The World is Ending Pass the Vodka' – makes me feel that I'm sitting at the bar already, watching the buildings topple across the street through the windows that will shatter any moment now. There is a sense of giving up in the face of insurmountable devastation with a sort of wry humour.

There are other images that stick in my mind too: the model of a pre-Columbian head with a perfect baby and cradle on top, made by a nine-year-old boy who was shot dead, in Sujata Bhatt's poem 'House of Silence' from her book *Pure Lizard*; Jane Griffiths' printer from the poem of the same name in her *Another Country*, when he appears to slam his car into a 'No Entry' sign in order to experience the lettering – and 'the weight of news in his palm' even as he becomes news.

It is no surprise that human relationships feature strongly as subject matter when a large number of poems are gathered together; despite widely disparate viewpoints this year's submissions are teeming with emotional considerations and observations of life.

Because human beings have first to deal with themselves before dealing with anything else, many of us are forever trying to work ourselves out – and everyone around us – and poets record this in their work using any object or metaphor at hand. Even discarded items or remnants are used as catalysts for this often forensic examination. In 'Past Caring' from Mick Imlah's collection *The Lost Leader*, he discovers the extent of a loved one's gin consumption when clearing out her house necessitates four trips to the bottle bank to unload the evidence. Now she is in a home 'too burgled to speak'. The gin bottles attach in my mind to the emotive image of an older relative (a mother or aunt?) and her loss of interest in life as the end of it approaches.

There are leftovers in the fridge from the poem 'Leftovers' in Kathryn Simmonds' book *Sunday at the Skin Launderette*, in which a solitary existence is described through the contents of the fridge against the backdrop of the differing lives of others in the same building, all concerned with the idea of a meal. I still recall the 'half a weightless aubergine'. I've always wondered at their lack of gravitational pull…

In 'Brothers', from Andrew Forster's collection *Fear of Thunder*, there is a left-behind brother, as the poet considers the effect of his youthful actions on the larger picture of his relationship with his younger sibling, when he is 'unable to close the distance' he'd set in motion – as if this distance has continued throughout their lives. In contrast, there is the small, intimate moment in Jamie McKendrick's poem 'An Encroachment', from his book *Crocodiles & Obelisks*, when he discovers a space at the other side of the bed with a woman's 'survival kit' tucked away in it. The creams and lotions describe the absent woman, and the poet's exploration of her decorative box with nothing in it increases the sense of trespass. Vignettes such as this can describe whole relationships, or act as a conduit for a small insight into something much greater beyond; just out of reach… these things fix themselves in the mind – my mind, in this instance.

The minds of my fellow judges, Fleur Adcock, Alan Brownjohn, Lemn Sissay and Natalie Whittle, were similarly affected, because once a book is digested a certain phrase, a particular line, or an individualised metaphor can bring back the impression that we formed of the thing as a whole. The imagery is what fastens the experience of reading the book – or a particular poem – into our memories. And when we sat down to work out the shortlist from our very, very long list, the memorable lines, images and ideas (often accompanied by copious notes) were what enabled each of us to argue the case for a book or a poem.

Without memorable imagery – or some element that stirs our senses into recognition – we are left with Teflon poetry that slides from the mind no matter how we try to cling to it. For us as judges, these non-stick poems and collections slipped from our grasp in the weeding-out process. Many other books and poems were harder to release, forcing an even closer examination of them between us. While we got a sense of each poet through their poems, we also got to know a little more of each other through our choices.

Sometimes a poem seemed designed to shock, but do such designs endear a poem to the reader any more than a fleeting pornographic image? Some poems asked questions, so we must question the questions. As with anything, it is always a case of how it is done.

Ultimately, our own questions about the poetry have to be answered, or there is no outcome; no winner. Is the poem – or the book of poems – memorable? Is it beautifully written? Does it have a point – or is it pointless? (Does it matter in any case?) Do we recognise/sympathise/empathise? Does it teach us anything? Or make us look at something that once seemed familiar in a different way? Do we like the language and/or imagery? Does it raise the hairs on the backs of our necks? Does it make us stop and consider? Does it move us in any way at all? Not all poems can do all things, and certainly not to all judges. In favourite poems there is usually a combination of some – but not often all – of the desirable elements, because it is rarely possible to please everyone simultaneously. However, I believe that the poems in this anthology represent the most comprehensive combination we could come up with. Choosing the final winners must be a distillation of this, but we have marvellous material to work with.

Our consolation in being unable to grant a prize of some kind to every book or poem we each saw as worthy, is this anthology. It includes two poems from each of the shortlisted books, all the shortlisted single poems and a poem from each of the books on the long list that the five of us brought to the table in the beginning.

If each book represents a poet's record of some of their inward and outward observations and their ruminations on the past from which they emerged, then one might imagine that each book is a little country – a country born of the individual poet's mind and experiences with its own rules, language and discoveries, which means that as judges we are extremely well-travelled. And as a guidebook through these new territories this anthology contains, I believe, stunning examples of the places to visit and the attractions that each country has to offer.

The Forward anthology is a fantastic showcase for the best of some of the most recent publications and the most talented of our new and established poets. Poetry anthologies should be, to my mind, the first introduction to poetry for any individual who is new to it and anyone uncertain of what might appeal to them. If choice breeds discernment and initiates discovery then this anthology is perfectly placed.

Thanks go to William Sieghart and his tireless efforts to make the writing of good poetry something to be applauded and rewarded, and for giving it a national stage in the form of the Forward Prizes. Huge thanks also to Kate Wright-Morris at Colman Getty, whose infinite patience (which must be sorely tried on some occasions!) and organisational skills make it all happen.

I am looking forward to meeting up with my fellow judges again in October, despite the fact that making our final choices is bound to cause us some grinding of teeth.

We hope that this anthology brings you as much pleasure – and some wonderful surprises – in the reading as it brought us in choosing the material.

Frieda Hughes, *August 2008*

Shortlisted Poems
The Forward Prize for Best Collection

Sujata Bhatt

WHAT IS EXOTIC?
for Hasso Krull

Sweden is exotic –
and so is all of Finland.

Whortleberries certainly are.

Estonia is exotic –
and so is the Estonian word
for lizard: *sisalik*.

But the lizard herself
is my sister – those hot afternoons
when she comes indoors
　　　　to hide –

A House of Silence
Medellín 2005

This is where the murderer meets
      the sister of his victim,
the wife, the children –

This is where they work,
side by side, not knowing
      who the other is.

Not allowed to speak, we're told,
they must speak with their hands,
they must make something out of clay.

A deaf-mute boy is the first
to greet us, fatherless at seven –
He places his sculpture in our hands:

A man and a woman in a tight embrace –
their spines cut deep as rivers
in their perfect, passionate backs.

Other children create clay figures
who are born chopped up – legs and arms,
torsos and even heads, lined up side by side.

The one I ask about is a pre-Columbian head
with a cradle on top, and a baby inside, intact –
I'm convinced it was made by an artist, a woman.

But no, I'm told, it was a boy of nine,
dead already, shot dead – and no one to claim his work.
Take it, they say, take it. Nobody wants it.

Jane Griffiths

Territorial

When the freeze came, we didn't think it strange.
It was the first winter in the new house, in
the new language. There were no known laws.

The small Renault driven out on the ice,
and the bonfire, were par for the course,
we thought; we saw straight through them

to the first house as it was with dark
glass set in white and knuckle-dusting walls,
before the burning. We learned to skate fast,

we saw the golden acrobatic fish frozen
under our dissecting blades, the triple-rimmed
eyes open, the stilled quiver of the scales.

We knew how to spin in our own body's compass
and how to vanish, floodlit, in a crowd.
We had by heart the geometries of ice:

the smooth black cross-hatched, pockmarked
brown and frothy white. The gunmetal crack
when it would bear, and the other silence.

We were fluent as the wind until we heard
of drowning, found our pathways undulating
soft as ash along the quick-backed waves.

The Printer

Years on, he remembers the letters,
the sense of them, at the very edge
of the fingertips of the mind:

the serifed slimness of *i* and *d*, ligatures
a hunch of shoulders jostling for position –
a *huffiness*. The small sharp hooks of *y*.

He knows the density of space and the diverse
parts of it: the em square, the makeweight
en, the mids and thins and the hair

a silver sliver, a catch in the breath.
He takes his morning paper wedged against
the marmalade, back to front and upside down,

can tell how *a* and *e* go neck and neck,
how the ampersand ends, how the comma
fits to a *t*. And he knows the frequencies –

why Russian stories went in italic,
the perennial scarcity of *k*. He can still
repeat his fingers' dance, analphabetic

over the orders of the tray, the slugs
of lead clicking home, home – but not
how he came here, hurtling into solid

space, slamming the brakes, at sixty,
for a No Entry sign not aimed at him
and wanting the sense of it, the ligature,

the weight of the news in his palm.

Jen Hadfield

Canis Minor

He lies in wait like a little headstone
as dry as dry as all Alberta.
I stop to pat his scrubby mohican.
His tongue spools out his head like magma.

Over the Jamieson place
the stars are rising through a peacock dusk
nice and steady in the arid air.

He scours his butt and licks my elbow.
He falls back on his haunches like a telescope,
winking and blinking his sunstung eyes.

Last light. Mosquito bite.
I scrounge a log from the Jamieson woodpile,
an armful of pinecones for kindling.

I put the fire in.
I begin to write this nice poem about your dog.

Odysseus and the Sou'wester

When Odysseus and his crew left his island, the King, Aeolus,
made him a final present – a fine breeze for the journey and the
leather haversack in which the rest of the winds were imprisoned,
warning him not to let anyone open the bag. Guess what...

I caught and oxtered it like a rugby ball,
a bloated bell of beating leather,
and for weeks I nannied the bloody thing –
on my lap, mending sails,
in a papoose, to climb the rigging.
When the boys got steamed on Aeolian wine,
I cuddled my squirming supper of winds –
let no one spell me for a wink of sleep.
From Aeolus to Malea was a waking dream.
Fat kingcups wobbled like boxing gloves.
With open eyes, I dreamt of home.
I clicked my heels in the blinking squill,
pillowed my skull on my second head,
and the boys said

                *oo*mpa-pa

    *oo*mpa-pa

                      Rockabye Baby!

as I dandled us home
on the sweet vesper gale.
*

Now the low, brown island strains on tiptoes,
and fences are strung with trembling streamers,
and the sea's mad as milk.

And my cheeks are scored with milky tears.
And like a puffball breaks the bag of winds.

And there's the Sou'wester,
a rising loaf of shuffled feathers,
struggling from the haversack
like a furious swan.

Mick Imlah

INKHORN

> *Il n'importe rien* – for export only

My part? – reciting the Seven Ages of Man,
with not enough *gusto*, apparently,
in an orange wig, while all around me rolls
'Time's Whirligig' – the Brownies doing cartwheels
over the forestage and the apron stage.

(If last year's show was a modest hit – 'Winston
at the Church Hall': I sang the Cliffs of Dover,
and the rest evolved from the sketches Geoff had kept
in mothballs from his salad days with ENSA
– the chemistry's not there with *Gloriana*.)

To help us round what Geoffrey calls
a little 'local difficulty', he proposes
that where in the final line the writer uses
French, 'sans eyes, sans teeth' (though pardon me,
dentures – didn't the Queen have a wooden set?),

we substitute *without* in each case, that way
it won't seem 'callous or condescending' (in my view,
should mine be wanted, the English softens the force).
They're charging five pounds to get in, but for
that you are also entitled to a buffet supper.

– Geoffrey, who would style himself Sir Walter,
and stars in a silent tableau of that knight
strolling along the prom at El Dorado
with a pipe and a baked potato, his tights worn
under a patent 'Hammond' or cricket box,

will swear – though he must be eighty, now – he once
saw a film called *Finish Your Bowls!*, in which
it was either Dietrich or Mae West – halted
on the half-landing and said, 'I may look like
a lady, but these are the bosoms of a *bitch*.'

The Ayrshire Orpheus

And down he went, sounding the deepest floors
Where Pluto ruled with serious Proserpine,
Still piping, till he reached their double doors
And knocked. And so he saw her, horribly thin:
Eurydice, her face all eaten in,
Curled at the feet of that disdainful pair
Who feigned surprise to see a Scotsman there.

Then Orpheus, soft and urgent, half in dread
Of what she had become: 'My bonny lass –
Hey – love – though it's better than being dead –
What's happened to your lovely lips and face?
How have they disappeared, or come to this?'
And she: 'Shoosh, pet, right now I dare not say –
But you shall hear the whole another day',

As Pluto intervened: 'Your silly wife
Has marred her face, and turned her belly barren,
Through dwelling on the home she may not have;
Mindful of Ballantrae and the view of Arran,
She finds the mills of Hell friendless and foreign;
If one could spring her now to the Ayrshire coast,
No doubt her looks would heal to their uttermost!'

So Orpheus sat before that mocking twosome
And let them have it, with his matchless voice,
Pitching 'Ye Banks and Braes' at the royal bosom;
A charming 'Ae Fond Kiss', and 'Ca' the Yowes',
And then 'My love is like a red, red rose';
Till Pluto swooned, and prickly Proserpine
Lay down her softening form upon the green.

The infernal lakes had filled with lily water,
Such was the gentle power of that recital,
When Pluto cleared his throat: 'I thank the Scot

Who wrote these songs, and you, who made them vital;
Name your own prize, and that shall be requital.'
And Orpheus begged, 'Then let me take my love
Back to that place we owned in the world above.'

Which tickled Pluto. – 'You're a bold one, Mac!
– Yet I'm inclined to grant such a request,
On this condition: should you once *look back*,
Your wife reverts to Hell of the heaviest!'
Then Orpheus clasped her freshening to his chest,
And up they strove, spiralling in their fate,
Till they had almost reached the outward gate.

If you have loved, imagine the sweet chat
The two then had, rejoining their own kind –
So can you blame him, in the midst of that,
If he should suffer a local lapse of mind?
I hate to say – she fell a yard behind –
Backward he blinked – chains belted from the deeps
And yanked Eurydice to Hell for keeps.

Poor Orpheus! He felt like some old town
Of Carrick in decline: Maybole, or Girvan,
The pubs shut down, the kids, taunting 'the clown
Who couldna face the front', on drugs from Irvine;
While dismal in the twilight of surviving
Alone with his shopping, sore to be rid of her,
He walks the roads of home a widower.

Jamie McKendrick

THE KEY

Janus two-faced god of folds and joints
hinges thresholds and enjambements
who has in his keeping lids locks doors
dawns dusks and all our various
exits and entrances it wasn't you
but Anastasio the old Salernitan
who handed me the key
the size of a cudgel its epic profile
wore holes in my secondhand raincoat
I then had to sew up with sackcloth
a cold iron tongue that should have turned
the stony earth or sprung the gates of Dis
but opened the vaulted flat that dated back
to the days of Torquato Tasso
in the street named after him.

Someone must be carrying that key
someone this late at night be walking through
the alleys past the Duomo's
bronze-nailed wooden door
up the worn steps with their rusted railings
stopping to drink from the slender wire that spills
out of the lion face's open mouth
in the small square awned by palm fronds
before feeling in their pockets for the key.

His brother who owned the key
that opened the flat with its vaulted ceiling
was in jail at Poggioreale Naples
since his lock-up
had been found full of semi-automatics
but Anastasio said his ignorance
was no defence against the law –

ma sì che era innocente … ci mancherebbe altro!

He unlocked the iron door to show the flat
blackened by the open brazier
the lacquers and gamboges that Enzo
the furniture restorer used
in the room with the balcony that overlooked
a sunken courtyard and a pomegranate tree
two Alsatians were chained to – a two-headed
Cerberus permanently hoarse
the only neighbours I ever saw
apart from a rat who gnawed at the bedroom door
geckoes suction-fixed to the ceiling
and scorpions who brandished claws
and twitched alembic tails in warning
like guardians of the underworld.

Anastasio gave me a tube of black glue
I never used to trap the rat
and in case I had doubts
the house he reminded me was *augurioso*
on account of the ex-convent opposite
no matter it was now a brothel
but didn't say the place would live in me
far longer than I lived in it.

The day he showed me round the flat
he lifted a marble slab in the floor
on a square of blackness and said beneath
there was another slab that opened on
one more square of black and so on down
past centuries of settlement
into the heart of the rock
until … and there he stopped unsure
but here's the key he said
I hope you're happy here.

Someone must be carrying the key
I still keep fishing in my pockets for
whose phantom weight
has left me bent or skewed
but maybe I never gave it back
it still turns anticlockwise in the lock
and opens a door as heavy as air
onto the dazzling dark on dark.

An Encroachment

Now I can take over your side of the bed
I discover the little space between
the bedside and the wall I'd been
unaware of – where you'd made

an installation like a survival kit:
biros specs nailfiles novels magazines
tubes of mild medicaments and creams
one decorative box with nothing in it.

I lift the nothing out and stare at it.
Never has nothing looked more splendid.
Fearful I've left a smudge and marred it
I quickly put it back and shut the lid.

Catherine Smith

SNAKEBITE
(i.m. Helen Penfold, 1961–1999)

Things are looking up. We've
found a pub where the landlord,
convinced by my smooth lies, your

proper breasts, will serve us snakebite.
He tips the lip of each pint glass,
froths in lager, pours cider and asks

How much blackcurrant, ladies?
You smile at him, murmur *When –*
we love how his hands shake

as you take your change.
We gulp like seasoned drinkers,
avoiding the stares of the old gits

with their bitter, their racing pages.
The drink hits the spot and
everything is funny. You nearly

take my eye out playing darts.
And at the Rec on the way home,
full of sugar and gas, we slump

on the swings we dared each other
to leap from as kids, jewelling
our palms and knees with grit.

We lean back under the night sky,
under all the stars we can't name,
we're full of how we'll leave

this dump of a town first chance we get –
how we despise the regular lawns,
the sagging paddling pools, we're

singing as we approach our road.
Today was hot, like the days,
buckling with laughter, we shoved

each other over on your drive,
the tarmac sucked at our sandals
and the ice-cream van played 'Lara'

from *Dr Zhivago*, too slow. Tomorrow
we'll feel sick as dogs. But tonight,
here, under a bright, full moon,

we're amazing, and as we hug
on my doorstep, I taste you,
kiss the snakebite off your lips.

Picnic

This way. He punches in the code;
five to midnight, the monitors glowing
like fish-tanks. The Veuve Cliquot
has roused them, their fingers
laced as he leads her to his manager's desk,
eases her clothes away like packaging,
kneels between her shaking legs.
She hardly murmurs even though
she's pressed against the in-tray –
this is an act of worship, but also unholy,
the desecration of the temple; the gods
will be angry with them forever.
Afterwards he asks *Are you hungry?*
They sit by the office fridge, and gorge
on Louise's strawberries, Geoff's garlic boursin,
Mary's half-bottle of Pinot Grigio.
They lick their fingers clean, kiss,
the cheese sweetening their breath.
She remembers her first picnic –
lemonade bubbles exploding in her mouth;
her mother's shoulders burned, thistles
pricking her through the wool blanket.
The songs in the long grass, swaying,
sandwich crusts curled in the heat
and the soft curdling of egg and cress.

Shortlisted Poems
The Felix Dennis Prize for Best First Collection

Simon Barraclough

Fusing the Braids

Three times a year you overhauled your hair,
firing the helical fuse that transformed
tightly-raked rows into electrical storms
of static and dandruff and ionised air.
Then, your black nimbus would radiate past
the edges of photos, pillows on beds,
reducing your face to a shrunken head,
leaving you other, untethered, distressed.
So for a weekend I became taboo
while expert fingers, with love, rebraided
the separate warring strands within you,
so I could return, all conflict evaded,
to pass a candle flame from tip to tip,
fusing hair and plastic, lip upon lip.

LONDON WHALE

Two journeys you took in your last two days:
the first unwisely swimming west and then
carried unluckily east in a poor sling,
a small red watering can barely wetting
the wrongheaded brow that saw fit to squeeze
you through the gate line of the Thames Barrier.
Just another morning commuter
touching in or out with an Oyster card.
If you were heading for work, what strange job, this?
Unbriefed ambassador, curious key
to some ancient chamber flooded with guilt,
or love, or the rattling blades of that bad old trade
which it seems never touched you. Why here and now,
you smiling stranger? Do they sing about the bones
in the old museum? Did you *have* to chance it?
Look how sentimental you make me;
we're a city of visitors, you see.

Andrew Forster

CHOOSING TO DISAPPEAR

It's just on odd mornings, at first.
His house is glossed by a different light.
Lines and edges sharpen. Chairs, tables,
drawers stand free of familiarity,
become mere objects on display.
His daughter's laughter, pearls tinkling,
is a memory he's trying to place.
His son has a face like the face
in the mirror whose contours he touches
as if testing a blade. And this woman,
his wife, her intimate smile speeds
his breathing, creeps from his skin like dew.
He shrugs it off with a routine
he wears like a suit, but it drips
into his consciousness, this feeling,
like a leaking pipe into a basin.

More and more he lingers
at chance meetings with strangers,
devours tiny details of other lives,
imagines being immersed in them
like a second skin, as if this would stop
his being outside himself, disbelieving
the life he lives, not remembering
how he arrived here. So he starts
a game, like a secret passion
for chocolate, something to sweeten
the days, make them easier to swallow:
money sliced off the joint account,
squirreled in a drawer beneath socks
and underwear, beside bus timetables
to places he's never been, or where
he spent holidays that fit like a glove.

From time to time his family notice
him looking at them without seeing,
but brush it away like mud trailed in a kitchen.
They're too caught up by their rush of days.
He does what he should, doesn't interfere,
so they carry his sometimes-silences
like a river grasping a fallen branch.
The kids slip into sleep warmed
by his stories of Narnia, oblivious
to his popping out to the late-night shop
and when he shoves the wad of notes
into his pocket, it means nothing:
just the game gone one stage further.
He checks that milk is all they need,
not sure why his token kiss lingers
on his wife's cheek, and he leaves.

She doesn't look at the time at first,
trying to piece together
a jigsaw-puzzle TV drama
and when all pieces are fixed in place
she curses the friends he must have met
and sips black coffee, impatience
measured by the hands of the clock.
Later, or the next day, she will look
for a trail on the rain-washed street:
check with the shopkeeper, question
staff at the local bar, phone around
unlikely acquaintances, consider the police
and that's it. There isn't an ending.
Just a litre of milk left behind
on a 305 bus, found
by a puzzled driver, about to go home.

THE HORSES

Our car coughs into the scrapyard, burning oil
smoking into the stillness of the lane.
You sign the document and that's it –
no point holding onto something that's dying.

Under a shifting roof of cloud we trudge
to the road. Chestnuts, elms and sycamores
strain with the weight of leaves, and rosebay
withers, its purple flowers yellowing

at the edges like pages of an old book.
Heading for the bus stop you turn, suggest
a walk. I shrug and we take the coastal path.
The harbour is deserted: a single boat,

paint flaking, is rocked on the water,
the empty clank of its rigging keeping time
with a half-hearted breeze. A gull takes off
from the crumbling wall with a clatter of wings.

Leaving the road, we climb down through gorse
to the beach. The clouds make space so the sun
can improvise something upbeat on my neck.
You quicken your pace and we sit on the sand.

The tide is in. Not far from the water's edge
the land must shelve, as the sea is suddenly
deeper. Two horses splash past us,
water lapping at their torsos. Their riders

lean back in their saddles, angling their boots clear.
The sun strokes the horses' flanks, picking out
shades of chestnut as they pull their freedom
from the sea's grasp, then slap their hooves

down again, moving on, shaking their manes,
showering silver spray into the air.
The riders' laughter hangs in the afternoon
as they let themselves be carried forward.

Frances Leviston

Dragonflies

Watching these dragonflies
couple in air, or watching them try,
the slender red wands
of their bodies tapped
end to end, then faltering wide
on the currents of what feels to me
a fairly calm day,

I think of delicate clumsinesses
lovers who have not yet mentioned
love aloud enact,
the shy hands they extend
then retract, the luscious fumbled chase
among small matters seeming massive
as rushes are to dragonflies,

and in the accidental
buzz of a dragonfly against bare skin,
how one touch fires
one off again on furious wings
driven towards love and love, in its lightness,
driven the opposite way,

so in fact they hardly meet
but hang in the hum of their own desires.
Still, who would ask
these dragonflies to land on a stone
and like two stones to consummate?
How can I demand love stop, and speak?

LAMPADROME

Lampadedromy n. (Gr. Antiq.)
A torch-race... 1848 Craig has the
incorrect form Lampadrome...
– OED

It's late, but here's the linkboy's light for hire.
He lifts it, dripping, high above his head,
and waits his corner, watching textures fade,
night flood the streets from its reservoir

submerging Corinth, and the men who pass
for a trading empire's living idols
in fur-lined cloaks and new leather sandals
grow nervous enough to approach him first.

There is a tremor inside their demands
for guidance – they know their silver palms
are dull as an abandoned temple's alms
without the benefaction of his brand,

which, with careless alchemy, transmutes
their muted coins and greying hair to gold.
Despite his advantage, he's still compelled
to mark the sought address and pick their route,

squeezing with awful calm through a dark door
his torch reveals to be the road, unpaved,
between the walls of housing so deprived
his passengers, for all they can be sure,

have shifted planes. They cling to the light,
not so much afraid of what they witness
as what their sudden consciences can guess –
the thieves and whores, the madman's single note –

must somewhere now be living, since they don't
appear to breathe the rest of Corinth's air.
Beyond the open doorway of a bar
full cups lie smashed, and women creak with want,

and some rough answer's blowing down the street.
The boy's a marvel! Completely unafraid,
and honest, too: his fee already paid,
he could – no loss – have left them there for meat,

but now they spill like syrup from a tap
and find they're on a thoroughfare they know,
carrying them round the lampadrome
past fans who press and crane at every gap.

Our boy is one. The merchants never guess
that every fare he's taken passed this way,
no matter what the risk, what loop awry
to skirt the roaring, monolithic mass

and through those columns' black interstices
to glimpse a distant nimbus – five, or six,
now clumped, now stringing out and out, like tricks
on the eyes – distending in a breeze

and lapping glory: fickle, minor gods
disguised at play, and each one's brazier hitched
to an athlete lit and lofted from the pitch
of obscurity – like Aaron's rod,

its roadside yellow flowers blazing high
to lead the funeral march through any map.
Applause unfolds inside, that sticky trap.
He'd like to run the race before he dies

or die right now, his unsung torch nipped out
and silver gone to get some bastard pissed.
What difference is there – linkboy, lampadist?
The one who burns within, the one without.

Allison McVety

and not. How you can know it
through your feet, through the pitch
and crack of pavement, through games:
their stones and sticks,
through hopscotch numbers
scratched on flags with chalk or coal.
Through the clip of ropes on kerbs,
the tap on grids, through the clap of hands,
the toll of dustbin lids, the spark
of studs on boots. Through Messerschmidt
and Spitfire arms, strobed or flecked
with rationed sun. How you can see a thing,
defined through shadows,
the twitch of nets, the very thick of it.
Through the snatch and flare
of two fags lit with the same match,
through the warden's bawl
to *put that bloody light out,*
to *shut the flaming door.* How one shell
can re-shape the place you know,
shift a shelter three feet north,
so you dig for the man in the tin hat
in the wrong place. And how
when they lift your father,
caked in dust, there are no cuts,
no bruises. This is how a man drowns
in earth, this is how you know a place.

Boy on the Bus

That school gabardine of mine
with its slip-in, slip-out lining,
quilted for winter use,
invisible brown on a bus of standard-issue.
Box-pleats and woollen tights knock knees
with overalls and Crimplene frocks.
In amongst the chiffon,
a crêpe-de-chine square on a shampoo and set.
One man in cavalry-twill, umbrella
tapping a tune on the soles of his brogues. And you
in army & navy surplus, air force blue,
collar raised and cocked, a knapsack
hanging from your shoulder
with the casual cool of *William Hulme*.
I never learned your name or saw you,
beyond your walk to an empty seat,
was never brave enough to look behind
or smile, but I felt you all the same.
Seventeen stops of feeling you.
Boy on the bus, I don't remember what happened
to my gabardine with its slip-in, slip-our lining,
its detachable hood, but I've seen your coat often
at fêtes, in second-hand shops, and once
in the cloakroom of the Festival Hall.
Each time, I've checked the label for your name,
the pockets for mine.

Stephanie Norgate

BIRTH

A story children love to hear
but can never remember.
'She was born on'… a biographer's note
that says nothing of the day in December
your sixteen-year-old mother and your father
struggle with the cold,
stopping the gaps in the plaster
with his granny's torn petticoat,
laying scarves and old socks
against the undercracks of doors,
lighting the gas which seeps
into running flames along each wall.

When you come slithering out,
they name you Myrtle
for the cottage which leaks fire and rain
while your mother sluices
herself down with water from the china jug
and your father fills his pipe
and worries and coughs
thinking how he really is a man
now he has a child. But you can't remember
any of it: Old Daise, your mother's stepmother,
embarrassing your mother
with a Romany blessing
and some eggs from the goose.

Before the six other children,
before the sixty-a-day Senior Service,
before the horses,
there is just you and them, and, after the rain,
winter sun whitens the old man's beard
which loops from beech to yew to beech

tracing the whole steep hill, and there is
your mother, bloody, and singing
with her long hair down,
the way you always wanted to remember.

The Phone Tower Wood

Out from under the phone towers, on quiet hooves,
    deer munch stems of Queen of the Night
before the tall, greening buds
    can ever uncup
their veined dusty crimson light,
    their pools of blood-black bruises.

It's a strange consolation to say, over and over,
    on the phone, or in pubs to city friends,
the deer have eaten the tulips again.
    On a rare evening, I'll see all three of them
cantering over the tussocky field,
    back to the phone tower trees and their humming cover.

Kathryn Simmonds

THE BOYS IN THE FISH SHOP

This one winds a string of plastic parsley
around the rainbow trout,
punnets of squat lobster and marinated anchovy,
the dish of jellied eels
in which a spoon stands erect.
He's young, eighteen perhaps,
with acne like the mottled skin of some pink fish,
and there's gold in his ear, the hoop of a lure.
The others aren't much older,
bantering in the back room,
that den of stinking mysteries
where boxes are carried.

The fish lie around all day,
washed-up movie stars
stunned on their beds of crushed ice.
The boys take turns to stare
through the wide glass window,
hands on hips, an elbow on a broom,
lost for a moment in warm waters until
Yes darling, what can I get you?
and their knives return to the task,
scraping scales in a sequin shower,
splitting parcels of scarlet and manganese.
Their fingers know a pound by guesswork,
how to unpeel smoked salmon,
lay it fine as lace on cellophane.
A girl walks past, hair streaming,
and the boy looks up,
still gripping his knife, lips parting in a slack O.

HANDBAG THIEF

Alone at last and you're unpacking everything:
the broken-spoked umbrella,
Plumbstruck lipstick, thriller
destined for a bin on Oxford Street.

Ignoring tissues and the half-popped
packet of Ibuprofen, which crackles
like lit tinder at your touch,
you seize the purse, transfer the twenties

cash point clean into the warm
back pocket of your jeans,
but leave the pennies and receipts,
the number of a man I met last week.

My telephone is ready for your speech,
befriend my friends or listen
to my voice apologise for failing
to pick up. The compact camera

fits your palm, you grin and turn
the last exposure on yourself,
a flash of teeth and bed-sit wallpaper.
We're floating in a dark room

side-by-side, my tan preserved between
your fingertips. Only when it seems
there's nothing left, unzip the inside
pocket and remove the poem scribbled

on an envelope: raise it like an X-ray
to the light. I'll leave you there
to finish it, chewing on my ballpoint,
drawing on my final cigarette.

Shortlisted Poems
The Forward Prize for Best Single Poem
in memory of Michael Donaghy

Christopher Buehlman

WANTON

The paparazzi got her
again outside the chip shop
next to her London hotel,
still drunk, the strap on one heel
undone, her dress wine stained,
once white, her hair
elf-locked, only this time
she looked at one
right through the lens of his camera,
came at him, her thighs
two columns, her lipstick
horrific
and he knew,
though he would only say once,
years later, piss drunk in Wales,
a cab driver now and his head shaved,
grey stubble coming in,
yes he knew
it was in fact a goddess,
a minor one, not Greek,
her name unpronounceable,
and he understood
that if he did not instantly
smash his camera
spectacularly on the ground
he could expect no kiss, no erection,
not even one look
from any woman, ever again
that did not suggest he had farted.
So of course he did it.
And the others took pictures of that,
and of her again, undressing,
walking away from them
and into the tube.

Seamus Heaney

CUTAWAYS

i
Children's hands in close-up
On a bomb site, picking and displaying
Small shrapnel curds for the cameramen

Who stalk their levelled village. *Ferrum*
And *rigor* and *frigor* of mouse grey iron,
The thumb and finger of my own right hand

Closing around old hard plasticine
Given out by Miss Walls, thumbing it
To nests no bigger than an acorn cup,

Eggs no bigger than a grain of wheat,
Pet pigs with sausage bellies, belly-buttoned
Fingerprinted sausage women and men.

ii
Or trigger-fingering a six-gun stick,
Cocking a stiff hammer-thumb above
A sawn-off kitchen chair leg; or flying round

A gable, the wingspan of both arms
At full stretch and a-tilt, the left hand tip
Dangerously near earth, the air-shearing right

Describing arcs – angelic potential
Fleetly, unforgettably attained:
Now in richochets that hosannah through

The backyard canyons of Mossbawn,
Now a head and shoulders dive
And skive as we hightail it up and away

iii

To land hard back on heels, like the charioteer
Holding his own at Delphi, his six horses
And chariot gone, his left hand lopped off

A wrist protruding like a waterspout,
The reins astream in his right
Ready at any moment to curb and grapple

Bits long fallen away.
The cast of him on a postcard was enough
To set me straight once more between two shafts,

Another's hand on mine to guide the plough,
Each slither of the share, each stone it hit
Registered like a pulse in the timbered grips.

Catherine Ormell

Campaign Desk, December 1812

I regret not giving it to my servant, Valentin,
when he went off saying it was his last blizzard;
for he left it with us on the field,
black as an olive, spotted with snow.

He was the one who'd wrapped it in a skin,
placed it on a cart half-Europe ago,
and between times, coaxed its legs out,
erected it, burnished it,
carried it under his arm like a cat.

Resourceful, well-loved Valentin;
who counted the hinges, praised the fixings,
kept them safe in his various pockets.

And while he considered it a drawing-room creature,
after Marengo I swear that desk bounced
under my nib like the plush rump of a mare;
at ease with the grass,
if sensitive to each volley of gunshot.

Most nights I wrote to a dancing troupe,
who were poor correspondents,
except for galloping Lalage;
she was always mirthful and tender.
I thought of anything but home,
despite the gift of my dear sister,

My God, even at war with Russia,
she sends me a portable schoolroom
to pen terrible icy letters to her;
and suggests Valentin might use it
to keep his scissors, his cheese safe.

Don Paterson

LOVE POEM FOR NATALIE 'TUSJA' BERIDZE

O Natalie, O TBA, O Tusja: I had long assumed the terrorist's
balaclava that you sport on the cover of *Annulé* –
which was, for too long, the only image of you I possessed –
was there to conceal some ugliness or deformity
    or perhaps merely spoke (and here, I hoped against hope) of a
young woman struggling
    with a crippling shyness. How richly this latter theory has
been confirmed by my Googling!

O who is this dark angel with her unruly Slavic eyebrows
ranged like two duelling pistols, lightly sweating in the pale light
of the TTF screen?
    O behold her shaded, infolded concentration, her
heartbreakingly beautiful face so clearly betraying the true focus
of one not merely content – as, no doubt, were others at the
Manöver Elektronische Festival in Wien –
    to hit *play* while making some fraudulent correction to a
volume slider
    but instead deep in the manipulation of some complex
real-time software such as Ableton Live, MAX/MSP
or Supercollider.

O Natalie, how can I pay tribute to your infinitely versatile
blend of Nancarrow, Mille Plateaux, Venetian Snares, Xenakis,
Boards of Canada and Nobukazu Takemura
    to say nothing of those radiant pads – so strongly reminiscent
of the mid-century bitonal pastoral of Charles Koechlin in their
harmonic bravura –
    or your fine vocals, which, while admittedly limited in range
and force, are nonetheless so much more affecting than the
affected Arctic whisperings of those interchangeably dreary
    Stinas and Hannes and Bjorks, being in fact far closer in spirit
to a kind of glitch-hop Blossom Dearie?

I have also deduced from your staggeringly ingenious
employment of some pretty basic wavetables
    that unlike many of your East European counterparts, all your
VST plug-ins, while not perhaps the best available,
    probably all have a legitimate upgrade path – indeed I imagine
your entire DAW as pure as the driven snow, and not in any way
buggy or virusy
    which makes me love you more, demonstrating as it does an
excess of virtue given your country's well-known talent for
software piracy.

    Though I should confess that at times I find your habit of
maxxing
    the frequency range with those bat-scaring ring-modulated
sine- bursts and the more distressing psychoacoustic properties
of phase inversion in the sub-bass frequencies somewhat taxing
    you are nonetheless as beautiful as the mighty Boards
themselves in your shameless organicizing of the code,
    as if you had mined those saws and squares and ramps straight
from the Georgian motherlode.

    O Natalie – I forgive you everything, even your catastrophic
adaptation of those lines from 'Dylan's' already shite
    Do Not Go Gentle Into That Good Night
in the otherwise magnificent 'Sleepwalkers', and when you
open up those low-
    pass filters in what sounds like a Minimoog emulation they
seem to open in my heart also.

    O Natalie: know that I do not, repeat, do not imagine you
with a reconditioned laptop bought with a small grant from the
local arts cooperative in the cramped back bedroom of an ex-
communist apartment block in Tbilisi or Kutaisi
    but at the time of writing your biographical details are
extremely hazy;
    however, I feel sure that by the time this poem sees the light of
day *Wire* magazine will have honoured you with a far more

extensive profile than you last merited when mention of that
wonderful Pharrell remix

was sandwiched between longer pieces on the notorious
Kyoto-based noise guitarist Idiot O'Clock, and a woman called
Sonic Pleasure who plays the housebricks.

However this little I have gleaned: firstly, that you are married
to Thomas Brinkmann, whose records are boring – an opinion I
held long before love carried me away –

and secondly, that TBA

is not an acronym, as I had first assumed, but Georgian for
'lake' – in which case it probably has a silent 't', like 'Tbilisi', and
so is pronounced *baa*

which serendipitously rhymes a bit with my only other word
of Georgian, being your term for 'mother' which is 'dada', or
possibly 'father' which is 'mama'.

I doubt we will ever meet, unless this somehow reaches you on
the wind;

we will never sit with a glass of tea in your local wood-lined
café while I close-question you on how you programmed that
unbelievably great snare on 'Wind',

of such brickwalled yet elastic snap it sounded exactly like a
12" plastic ruler bent back and released with great violence on
the soft gong

of a large white arse, if not one white for long.

But Natalie – Tusja, if I may – I will not pretend I hold
much hope for us, although I have, I confess, worked up my
little apologia:

I am not like those other IDM enthusiasts in early middle age; I
have none of their hangdog pathos, my geekery is the dirty secret
that it should be

and what I lack in hair, muscle-tone and rugged good looks I make
up for with a dry and ready wit ... but I know that time and space
conspire against me.

At least, my dear, let me wish you the specific best:
may you be blessed
with the wonderful instrument you deserve, with a 2 Ghz
dual-core Intel chip and enough double-pumped DDR2 RAM
for the most CPU-intensive processes;
then no longer will all those gorgeous acoustic spaces

be accessible only via an offline procedure involving a freeware
convolution reverb and an imperfectly recorded impulse
response of the Concertgebouw made illegally with a hastily-
erected stereo pair and an exploded crisp bag
for I would have all your plug-ins run in real-time, in the
blameless zero-latency heaven of the 32-bit floating-point
environment, with no buffer-glitch or freeze or dropout or lag;
I would also grant you a midi controller of such responsiveness,
such smoothness of automation, travel and increment
that you would think it a transparent intercessor, a mere
copula, and feel machine and animal suddenly blent.

This I wish you as I leave Inverkeithing and Fife
listening to *Trepa N* for the two hundred and thirty-fourth
time in my life
with every hair on my right arm rising in non-fascistic one-
armed salutation
towards Natalie, my Tba, my Tusja, and all the mountain
lakes of her small nation.

Kate Rhodes

Two months, they said
or with luck factored in, up to a year.
By then you'd abandoned luck,
decided to throw a party immediately.

It would last all weekend
in your favourite place –
a gaggle of caravans
hidden behind the dunes.

We waited for guests in our tin box,
rain clog dancing on the roof.
It took two boxes of matches
the best part of an hour, to light the fire

and I wanted to tell you
I can't do this. I can't celebrate
knowing you, then losing you
before you've even finished school.

But you were lolling on a pile of cushions
head back, listening to the sea.
Come and sit by the mirror, you said.
I'm going to show you

how to do your eyes.
You'll see how easy it is,
and when I'm finished
you won't know yourself.

Tim Turnbull

ODE ON A GRAYSON PERRY URN

Hello! What's all this here? A kitschy vase
some Shirley Temple manqué has knocked out
delineating tales of kids in cars
on crap estates, the Burberry clad louts
who flail their motors through the smoky night
from Manchester to Motherwell or Slough
creating bedlam on the Queen's highway.
Your gaudy evocation can, somehow,
conjure the scene, without inducing fright
as would a Daily Express exposé,

can bring to mind the throaty turbo roar
of hatchbacks tuned almost to breaking point,
the joyful throb of UK garage or
of house imported from the continent
and yet educe a sense of peace, of calm –
the screech of tyres and the nervous squeals
of girls, too young to quite appreciate
the peril they are in, are heard, but these wheels
will not lose traction, skid and flip, no harm
befall these children. They will stay out late

forever, pumped on youth and ecstasy,
on alloy, bass and arrogance and speed
the back lanes, the urban gyratory,
the wide motorways never having need
to race back home, for work next day, to bed.
Each girl is buff, each geezer toned and strong
charged with pulsing juice which, even yet,
fills every pair of Calvin's and each thong
never to be deflated, given head
in crude games of chlamydia roulette.

Now see who comes to line the sparse grass verge,
to toast them in Buckfast and Diamond White,
rat-boys and corn-rowed cheerleaders who urge
them on to pull more burn-outs or to write
their donut O's, as signature, upon
the bleached tarmac of dead suburban streets.
There dogs set up a row and curtains twitch
as pensioners and parents telephone
the cops to plead for quiet, sue for peace –
tranquillity, though 's, only for the rich.

And so, millennia hence, you garish crock,
when all context is lost, galleries razed
to level dust and we're long in the box,
will future poets look on you amazed,
speculate how children might have lived, when
you were fired, lives so free and bountiful
and there, beneath a sun a little colder,
declare How happy were those creatures then,
who knew that Truth was all negotiable
and Beauty in the gift of the beholder.

Highly Commended Poems
2008

Patience Agbabi

Eat Me

When I hit thirty, he brought me a cake,
three layers of icing, home-made,
a candle for each stone in weight.

The icing was white but the letters were pink,
they said, *EAT ME*. And I ate, did
what I was told. Didn't even taste it.

Then he asked me to get up and walk
round the bed so he could watch my broad
belly wobble, hips judder like a juggernaut.

The bigger the better, he'd say, *I like*
big girls, soft girls, girls I can burrow inside
with multiple chins, masses of cellulite.

I was his Jacuzzi. But he was my cook,
my only pleasure the rush of fast food,
his pleasure, to watch me swell like forbidden fruit.

His breadfruit. His desert island after shipwreck.
Or a beached whale on a king-size bed
craving a wave. I was a tidal wave of flesh

too fat to leave, too fat to buy a pint of full-fat milk,
too fat to use fat as an emotional shield,
too fat to be called chubby, cuddly, big-built.

The day I hit thirty-nine, I allowed him to stroke
my globe of a cheek. His flesh, my flesh flowed.
He said, *Open wide*, poured olive oil down my throat.

Soon you'll be forty ... he whispered, and how
could I not roll over on top. I rolled and he drowned
in my flesh. I drowned his dying sentence out.

I left him there for six hours that felt like a week.
His mouth slightly open, his eyes bulging with greed.
There was nothing else left in the house to eat.

Moniza Alvi

THE CROSSING

God, or someone, had parted the sea, and who were we
to say we weren't going to walk through it?

The cliff-like corridor, its glassy walls. We didn't dare
speak in case the great lift-doors of the earth would close

and drown us – feared to touch the translucent sides,
shells and seaweed fixed to a screen.

Fish stared, large as cabins, small as fingernails:
the knife-like, the black funereal, the bridal-tailed.

We moved as one, as surely as if we'd sponsored
each other. And those of us at war with ourselves,

our different parts were fused together.
We were twinned with our own undulating faces.

Who could know how our dire and honourable world
would re-establish itself?

The sky was below us and the sand above us.
Bitter as chocolate, the east wind blew all night.

Simon Armitage

from OUT OF THE BLUE

4
Arranged on the desk
among rubber bands and bulldog clips:

here is a rock from Brighton beach,
here is a beer-mat, here is the leaf

of an oak, pressed and dried, papery thin.
Here is a Liquorice Allsorts tin.

A map of the Underground pinned to the wall.
The flag of St George. A cricket ball.

Here is calendar, counting the days.
Here is a photograph snug in its frame:

this is my wife on our wedding day,
here is a twist of her English hair.

Here is a picture in purple paint:
two powder-paint towers, heading for space,

plus rockets and stars and the Milky Way,
plus helicopters and aeroplanes.

Jelly-copters and fairy-planes.
In a spidery hand, underneath it, it says,

'If I stand on my toes can you see me wave?'

Annemarie Austin

Avoided Subject

What I am avoiding will not be in this poem.
But you know the war museum is right below
the clouds Cornelia Parker photographed
with the camera of Hoess of Auschwitz –
whom we suppose more likely to have snapped
fields of buttercups than gas chambers.
I pressed the vetches picked from between
preserved huts at Birkenau, but also entered
each long darkness pungent with the chemicals
that kept woodrot at bay. They were needed –
the ground was boggy in August – but that phrase
is compromised in the context, it's as if
I'm meaning something else. Menace is a given,
though the fear of crime's far worse, they say,
(for now and for us) than statistics justify.
The house next door stood unoccupied for months
and no one broke in to rummage through
the displayed possessions – clothes and cooking pots
and spectacles and satchels not in glass cases.
Combing my hair at the window, I watch for
thunderheads to rise above the seaward roofs
loaded with hail that falls out of the chimney
onto my hearth as fat spots of liquid soot.

Bob Beagrie

THE LINESMAN

This morning's so primed for living
or dying, you must remember to wear
a Superman top under your shirt;
for you met, last night, a man named Lorry
The brother of a friend's ex-girlfriend,
who was once a driver in the army
and always went on the sick
rather than go to war with the nifty trick
of popping his hip joint out of its socket.
Saw his mates come back damaged, not fit
for anything anymore. So when he left
he became a linesman, climbing pylons,

Been electrocuted dozens of times,
As long as you're not grounded you can handle it
it's the best job in the world, up there
in the Outer Hebrides, in all weathers
· in France, on the west coast of Ireland
where on a clear day you can almost spot America
and all hangovers are shed on the climb
and the money's great and there's travel,
good crack and lots of fine women
and I've fallen dozens of times in the past,
Mostly I've bounced, but last time
I landed on concrete and broke both my legs.
Doctors said I'd never walk again,
but eighteen months later I'm walking fine.
I could have sued, but I'd never work again.
I've tortured myself in the gym
and snapped a steel pin in one leg
but eighteen months later – I'm walking fine
and waiting for a doctor to sign the form

that says I can go back to work, get back there
cos it's the best job there is, among the lines,
and when you've climbed through the frosty web
to see the sunrise, you're the king of the world.

Pat Borthwick

The Widower's Button

I asked you for thread and needle
to repair our sudden heat
but her straw sewing basket
(pink raffia flowers, a butterfly)
contained all your married years:
the children's woven name tapes,
her suture scissors, the repair kit
from a hotel in Beijing.
Odd buttons and press studs
fastening the four of you together.

She must have used this same needle,
this same white thread,
easing them along cotton hems,
newly laundered shirts,
the smell of sheets fresh from the line.

I was to have sewn your white button on,
but instead I am threading gaps
into a patchwork
whose pattern I can only glimpse
through photographs and ornaments,
the bathroom shelf,
what I imagine behind those wardrobe doors.

I take up her embroidery:
a perfect lawn in variegated strands,
feather stitch and satin stitch,
lazy daisies along an unfinished path.
It's left with the threaded needle in
as if the phone had rung
or she'd gone to put the kettle on.

You bring me a cup of tea,
watch me flounder with the button.
The needle's point
refuses to come up through the hole.
The cotton twists back on itself,
ends up in knots
I have to tease out gently,
knowing that if I try too hard
I might slip and prick my finger,
snap the thread.

Sue Boyle

A Leisure Centre is Also a Temple of Learning

The honey coloured girl in the women's changing room
is absorbed in making her body more beautiful:
she has flexed and toned every muscle with a morning swim
and showered away the pool chemicals
using an aromatic scrub and a gentle exfoliant.

Lithe as a young leopard, she has perfect bone structure;
her breasts mound as though sculptured from sand by a warm wind;
her secret cleft is shaved as neatly as a charlatan's moustache.

In dreamy abstractedness she applies cream,
then spray perfumes every part that might be loved.
Her long hands move in rhythm like a weaver's at a loom –
tipped throat, underchin, the little kisspoints below her ears
the nuzzle between her breasts, her willow thighs.

Her head tilted like a listening bird
she brushes her hair so whistle clean it is like a waterfall.

A bee could sip her.
She is summer cream slipped over raspberries.
She is so much younger than the rest of us –

she should look around.

We twelve are the chorus:

we know what happens next.

Lawrence Bradby

THE PORT

On a coastal ledge backed by high white cliffs,
which are not white but rising green,
reticulated cast iron balconies bleed rust
down the pale frontage of hotels,
which are not hotels but emergency accommodation
housing short stay clients,
who are not clients but subjects of the money, agents, chance,
their own tenacity
which bore them through tight conduits with Europe's roaring
                                      freight
to this safe country,
which is not safe but undecided,
so it stalls them
on this doorstep backed by high green cliffs
like sour milk
while it supervises slumping mounds of forms
handwritten
with versions of their lives laid out
precisely as required
showing the unique chronology
of their horrors
which are not horrors but the usual inhumanities, banal,
classifiable,
which gets the clients nowhere,
which is here
where the wind gnaws at the gantries and the ferries, like sudden
                                    building sites,
come up too close.
This is no emergency. It is the routine of the port.

Colette Bryce

THE KNACK

Place yourself
between the tracks, lie

as you would occupy
a grave – arms

crossed on chest, eyes
closed, deep

breath – and the life
will thunder over.

Wait through screech
and wheeze of brakes,

billow of smoke,
dust, heat,

for a settling.
Get to your feet.

If a hand is offered
from above, take it

with good grace; climb
back into the afternoon

and the next phase.

John Burnside

> *And your solitude will bear immense fruit in*
> *the souls of men you will never see on earth.*
> – Thomas Merton

1 Our Marital Selves

Like something that runs
forever beyond our keeping,
this silent movie on the LCD
unspools, while we go on with something else;

no bells to toll, no promises to keep,
their candlelight, and summers at the lake,
stacked in a cupboard, golden, or solid white
in that yellowish glow we choose to mistake
for knowledge;

       how they walk home in the snow
and stand at the kitchen table, ignoring the phone,
remembering minus or π
in the milk of a textbook;

how, every night, the house is folded up
and put away;

       and how, in the foregone conclusion
of ache, or departure,
they never look back, although they are grateful
for this
    like the life neverending:

one thing for sure in a future they cannot dismantle,
barley fields blurring to stone, then the silver of autumn,
bones in the bridal dress, fragments of shell in the icing.

2 Women in Photographs

Because they know exactly what to do,
scrubbing a table down, or wrapping a corpse
in coal-tar and Sunday best;
                                        because they wait
so perfectly, in sculleries that smell
of bleached sheets, or the memory of liver,

they seem the private versions of a life
we thought of years ago, but set aside
for later: quiet, L-shaped narratives
of washrooms, and the hum of terminus
that waits all afternoon to be admitted;

women with empty faces, pocked with light,
girls in their later years, their dreams of harvest
folded and put away in attic rooms

with vanished children, trinkets, windfall plums
and long-dead husbands, cleansed, then laid to rest,
like innocents, before the staggered dark.

3 Amour De Soi

Like saying a thing, then knowing it is true,
this private love, that smoothing out the lines
of self-regard;
                        flowers or rain in the mirror, the windows
filling with the blaze of early spring

and, all the time, that absence in the glass
coming to life as gaze, or the near recognition
that keeps the soul on track;

how, sometimes, going out,
you meet yourself coming in
from a different weather,

rain on your sleeves, or the white of japonica
lighting your face, when you turn and the shadows are what
they ought to be – no black, and no hidden caesura,

even if what you see has the transitive air
of something already known: not the fog of possession
but everything given up, or revised, or forgotten
to live *in* the present, not *for*, and the moment unending.

4 The Turing Test

I could have wakened
in a house like this,
hearing the wind arrive
at a turn in the stairs,

rabbits, there, or
something like a badger,
owls in the slur
from one thought to the next;

buzzard-light, rat-light,
skewed across a wall,
whole families of muntjac
stopping to prove
the absolute of snow
against a door;

witch-hazel, meadow,
raptures of fox in a passing
headlamp
as it drifts across the floor

and, somewhere behind it all,
suggested, *sub voce,*

the animal
that I might still become
if I walked to the end
of the hallway and entered
the one room of nothing but grasses:
timothy, fescue, quaking grass, silky agrostis,
feathering into the light
like the thought of forever.

5 Bethany

Waking at 3 a.m. is becoming an art;
an art, or a gift, delivered through sleep and quiet,

parcels of snow and sky
from another country,

lights from a childhood that feels
so recent, we might not have aged at all.

Give us this day, we say, and continue
moving the pieces, trying to puzzle it out,

a picture of fog, or stars, through an open window,
hares in the long grass, mice in the folds of the yard,

the wisp of sun unfurling from a wall
that matches us

for warmth and transience,
the fabric of a life, asleep and waking,

finding and losing its way
in the house of the echo.

6 On the Border

For afterlife, I'll wake in a motel
near Ajo, in some inexpensive room
with furniture that looks like *trompe l'oeil,*

the smell of the desert, cholla and creosote,
trapped in the clothes I have folded across a chair,
the TV like a mute child by the door

waiting to see what will happen when the wind
unfolds through the room like the angel of the lord
in a *quattrocento* painting: citrus and leaf-green

traces in the shape I take for wings
and enter, as if discovered, or silently claimed

by the grammar of morning,
the yellow, unspeakable Word.

Stephen Burt

PEONIES

       Yes, another
poem about flowers and kids. Our son
       thinks this one is a ball,
or full of balls: like jesters' caps with bells,
one for each stem, or old pawnbrokers' signs,
the lot next door in rainy April weather
dangles, and then in sunlight lifts, what he
believes he ought to pluck and grasp and throw,

if we would let him. Little does he know
       how each bud, given cues
from symbiotic ants, will open up
pink surface after surface, flagrant scraps
of incandescent fabric coming loose
like grown-ups' lives or last month's local news,
like promises, or generosity,
or overuse. So soon it isn't fair,

what he could take in his small fist all spring
and shake in anger when we told him no –
that is, *don't touch them* – nods, and will agree
to share its colours: still unravelling,
       curled up against its core,
each of the heavy flowers starts to be
a casualty of gravity, so low
it looks ashamed, as if the earth expected more.

Ciaran Carson

L'Air du Temps

That whiff of L'Air du Temps I got back then in the wardrobe –
I remember when I first registered that primal scent,

whence the symbolism of the pair of intertwining doves,
and the frosted glass bottle that made you think of Paris

under a cloudless winter sky, as I did of your blouse
of pale pastel blue, so crisp and clean and near transparent.

Then it began to develop waves, and I was standing
with you on a beach as we noted how the laps of foam

mouthed upon one another, how the crest of the barrel
doubled and broke into a shrubbery of jumping sprays.

We got soaked with spindrift and spray, our cheeks frosted with
    brine,
but we saw the waves well. In the sunlight they were green-blue,

flinty sharp, and rucked in straight lines by the wind, bottle-green
under their forelocks, or the turned-over plait of the crest.

The laps of running comb buffeting the sea wall doubled
on themselves, plied and purled in their folded crash and back-swash,

clocking the stones underwater against one another.
We leaned unsteadily into the wind all the way back

to the hotel. We stood and looked at the waves for a while
from the bay window. We switched off the lights to watch TV.

They were showing the latest news from my native city.
It looked like a Sixties newsreel where it always drizzled,

the police wearing glistening black ulsters and gun-holsters.
When it came to the bit with the talking heads we switched off.

We must have drifted off to the far-off sound of the waves,
both of us thinking of how, when taking off your jersey

of rib-knitted wool in the dark, with an accidental
stroke of your finger you drew a flash of electric light.

Angela Cleland

PEELING

One potato. Four minutes late:
you lost your car in a sea of cars.

Two potato. Five minutes:
the dark and the frost beat you to it –
it took a while to get the old girl started.

Three potato. Six minutes:
you hit a rabbit, had to get out,
check the bumper, check the rabbit.
She didn't want to start again.

Four. Seven minutes late:
braking on black ice you slid
like butter on a hot bonnet
into the back of a Merc; you are
exchanging details with a beautiful woman.

Five potato. Eight minutes:
you swerved and lost control.
Your car is wrecked, being towed,
your phone – you left it in the office,
the rabbit's dead, the other car's totalled,
torn wide open like a corned-beef tin.

Six potato. Nine minutes:
the two cars are twisted
round each other like sweetie wrappers.
You are still trapped inside
while firemen try to cut you out.
They cannot hear above the screaming
metal, you begging them to call me.

Seven potato. Ten minutes:
no one else was there when it happened,
no one saw you slither from the road
in disastrous elegance. You are trapped,
your phone… you left it in the office.
No other cars pass, not a soul,
not even the rabbit sees you lying
unconscious. No one will find you until…

More. More than ten minutes late:
there has been a freak landslide,
the cars are pinned together
and the woman in the Merc – no,
an earthquake, an explosion,
the next ice-age – a meteor
has torn the tarmac from beneath you.
The firemen can't get to your car,
the frost, corned-beef, the rabbit, you are –

the phone rings, the knife slips on wet peel,
slices my finger with ease; the taste
is sweet, warm, fast on my lips,
as I walk to the phone, lift the receiver.

Robert Crawford

FULL VOLUME

Diving-suited, copper-helmeted, no thought of turning back,
Led by his grey lead boots way, way off the beaten track,

He walks into Loch Ness. His unheard wife and daughter
Stand hand-in-hand on the shore. Underwater,

He ploughs on down on his own, bone-cold marathon,
Stomping the loch not for any sponsorship he's won,

Not seeking front pages, nor getting caught up in some blinding
Damascus flash, but just for love of that dark, reminding

Him and his folks here and all the folks
Back home that, despite the old jokes,

Hoaxes, photos, no-shows, and tourists' tales,
Something is in there, out there, down there, flails and dwells

In inner silence. He wants to meet
It, to come back dry, dripping, and greet

The day from the loch's beyond, its call
Calling inside him. Wants above all

To sound the loch's full volume right at ground
Level, be lost in it, pushed by it, sung by it, not to be found.

Bernadette Cremin

Nadia

keeps a bunch of razors
tidy with a tartan scrunchie

has let talcum settle
on a jar of clouded bath oil

and kept the black chiffon bow
from a cheap bottle of French shampoo

and is content to let oatmeal soap sit
in the same milk-puddle for months

has left a tub of crushed apricot stone
and horse chestnut scrub to crust

into a cluster of scabs
around the rim and under the lid.

Sometimes Nadia stares for too long
into the frosted pot of lilac balm

that sits in the middle of the sill
like a spoiled princess.

J P Dancing Bear

Natural Enemies

all day the owl is dreaming of a crow, dreaming
of a crow, dreaming of a crow and his war caw
rushing through the pines, and the owl opens
her mouth as if to say wait, wait until nightfall,
until nightfall when the crow's own blackness
is not enough to hide him from her keen eyes.

all night the crow is dreaming of an owl, dreaming
of an owl, dreaming of an owl and battle screech
so close it could run through his dark body and sever
his spine. his mouth moves in silence: wait, wait
until daybreak when the owl's gray camouflage
cannot protect her from the murders of crows.

in twilight the owl and crow are praying to live, praying
to live, praying to live the long hours of hunting. they do
not fly nor tempt the other into the unowned time
and orange territory of conflicted light. they bide, bide
in their pine churches with their psalms to a god
who would favor their feathers over the other's.

Isobel Dixon

Meet My Father

Meet my father, who refuses food –
pecks at it like a bird or not at all –
the beard disguising his thin cheeks.
This, for a man whose appetite was legend,
hoovering up the scraps his daughters couldn't eat.

The dustbin man, we joked.
And here he is, trailing his fork
through food we've laboured to make soft,
delicious, sweet. Too salty, or too tough,
it tastes of nothing, makes him choke,
he keeps insisting, stubbornly.
In truth, the logic's clear. His very life
is bitter and the spice it lacks is hope.
He wants to stop. Why do we keep on
spooning dust and ashes down his throat?

Maura Dooley

THE FINAL STAGES OF DIPLOMACY
Dick Cheney, March 2003

On the asphalt they argue about positions,
one puts down a bag to mark the spot,
the next wants to know what is in the bag.
Someone else comes now, stands silently,
saying nothing, his hands loose at his sides,
he says nothing, and then they start to push.

We make our little murmuring noises
of restraint, we smile or look anxious.
It goes on and it is the bag's fault,
this pushing. If only someone
would open the bag (Look! Empty!)
or take it away, it doesn't need to be there.

If only the bell would go.

If only Sir would come,
(nonchalant, only slightly late)
to usher them inside, orderly,
the bags all checked and safely stowed,
then Circle Time on the carpet,
Show and Tell, prayers.

Stephen Dunn

REPLICAS

When it became clear aliens were working here
with their dead-giveaway, perfectly cut Armani suits,
excessive politeness, and those ray guns
disguised as cell phones tucked into their belts,
I decided we had two choices: cocktail party
to befriend them, or massive air strikes (I joked
at the Board meeting) on what might be a hospital
for children with rare diseases, but could
as easily be where these aliens spawned and lived.
Cocktail party it was, and they came
with their gorgeous women dressed like replicas
of gorgeous women, and though they sipped
their martinis as if they'd graduated
from some finishing school between their world
and ours, I must admit they were good company,
talking ball scores and GNP, even movies,
and how bright and inviting the stars seemed
from my porch. I found myself almost
having sympathy for what certain people will do
to fit in, until I remembered they might want
to take over, maybe even blow things up.
And when the dog barked from the other room,
the way she does when some creature is nearby,
about to cross an invisible line, I was sure
I couldn't afford to trust appearances ever again.
Then it was time to leave, and they left,
saying at the door what a good evening they'd had.
Each of them used the same words,
like people who've been trained in sales,
and as they moved to their Miatas and Audis
I noted the bare shoulders of their women
were the barest shoulders I'd ever seen,
as if they needed only the night as a shawl.

Mark Ford

SIGNS OF THE TIMES

'Today,' wrote Thomas Carlyle
As the brown and barge-laden Thames rolled past
Cheyne Walk, 'I am full of dyspepsia, but also
Of hope.' On the *Today*
Show today a dyspeptic interviewer set brusquely about
A hopeful minister, and I ingested, along with the dyspepsia
And the hope, a story about a dubious collector
Of Regency soft toys and Apache
Bows, arrow-flints and tomahawks. Next
In line to be scalped was a corrupt
TV game-show host. Whither
The gentle, humane
Quizmaster-ship of Magnus Magnusson, or the calm and
                                            bespectacled
Bamber Gascoigne?
                        Sweet day, so cool, so calm,
So bright, on which I don a shirt that cries out
For cufflinks, and sports
Embroidered initials on the right-hand cuff; on
Which I opened a desk-drawer and discovered
A dozen or so pairs of sun-, half-rim-, and reading-glasses
Beneath an essay in progress on the French
Revolution, and notes
Towards another on the Spanish Civil War. We
Were born in the forward-
Thinking Sixties, and grew up in various capital cities in Africa
And Asia – wherever, that is, the British Overseas Airways
                                     Corporation
(BOAC, for short) saw fit. In Lagos
The gardener earned a trifling bonus for each
Black mamba he destroyed
With his machete: they lurked mainly in the cool
Of the garage, curled behind the whitewall

Tyres of our sturdy Zephyr, deaf to the shouting and rifle-fire
Of the barracks adjacent, and military sirens tearing
Open the heavy heat.
                              It took – or seemed
To take – no time at all for the venom to prove, point
By careful point, what it meant. I found
Myself sweating too, trying
To recall the serpentine journeys made by adventurers such as
                                                  Mungo Park
And Richard Burton, and the weeping jungles
And empty deserts they traversed. Unsheathed, their bone-
Handled bush knives whispered
Like settling locusts or long-
Promised waterfalls. One sticky morning
John Hanning Speke awoke on a spur above Lake
Tanganyika with a ferocious headache,
Blind as an earthworm. The clear lake waters rippled
And sighed, then flared like a peacock's tail beneath the
                                          whitening sky.

Adam Foulds

5 Night Fires

Two bodies in the tree.

Home Guards touched them
with their torch beams,
feeling their way up
to the popped faces.
Two loyalist elders:
a headman and his brother.
Someone found where one rope
was tied to the trunk
and hacked through.
The headman dropped vertically
onto his heels, bounced, landed
again, sank sideways, staring.

Careful. Please.

Sir, do you hear something?

The sergeant, realising:
Who told us to come here?
Who told us this was here?

                    *

The patrol pulled into the sergeant's own village
to see it almost finished. No one screaming.
The men labouring hard, quietly, as in a workshop,
a boat builders' yard,
limbs and parts scattered around them,
their wet blades in the flamelight
glimmering rose and peach.
The wheezing collapse of a burning hut,

its final volley of sparks, inches long,
snapping through greasy blackness, into nothing.
The sergeant emptied his revolver,
spun one man onto the ground.
The others flashed like fish and disappeared.

After them!

*

Tom sat for the first time
on the glimpsed adult furniture
of the gentlemen's bar
of the East Highlands Country Club.
Creaking maturity of wood and leather.
Marine, meditative drifts of cigar smoke
wandering around him. He hurried
its blue curves with his own breath
while the men talked.

                   And the men talked.
Tom's accession could hardly distract them.
His father's introductions
grew more buttonholing, hucksterish.

Talk was of Frank Grayson and Charles Hewitt,
the two old boys who dined together,
clobbered by their own servants,
just absolutely butchered.
And there were other incidents –
everyone had something from his own farm.
And the Governor was *no more use
than a margarine dildo.*

Tom had had a nightmare the previous night:
he and Kate in the corridor
down to matron's room,
building a barricade of chairs,
permeable, collapsing, clatteringly rebuilt,

which wouldn't keep anybody out.
Aside from that, he'd found it hard to fear
consistently. At home he kept forgetting.
Everything looked so much as always,
the objects placid, the weather, the days like others.
Here among these men who'd simmered
for weeks in their adrenalin,
his own fear took shape, hardened,
with edges, between his lungs.

No one really spoke to him.
Prior of the KPR was there
and closest to Tom's age
but he spoke to no one,
or nodded at what Jenkins said.

In the panelled room
the men's tans looked wrong.
Nervy, thickening, strained,
their faces looked dirtied by the sun.
Unsettled: they'd thought their major war over.
Sitting by Tom's father, Monty Parker's
face had a cracked glaze,
white crows' feet showing through.
One of the old set,
his vigorous enterprise
with other men's wives might not
have surprised Tom if he'd been told.
He remembered him jogging
round a pool in dripping trunks,
smiling out to his incisors,
instigating games.

You bunking up here tonight?

Tom answered, his father watching:
We weren't planning on it.

Monty leaned back, slid
his palms down his chest.
I suppose it's not too far for you.
I will. MMBA for me to get back.
Then unpacked the familiar slang
with leisured loathing:
Miles and miles of bloody Africa.

A message for Jenkins pulled him from the room.
It looked urgent.
Trouble in the nursery
got no laughs.

When he returned, he was followed
by a Home Guard Johnny
who loitered by the door
unaware of his audacity,
breathing hard, in a filthy uniform,
shoes splashed, Tom noticed, and not with mud.

Jenkins stood in the middle of the room.
Gentlemen, there's a hunt on.
There's been a ferocious carve-up,
maybe a hundred loyalists are dead.
The Mau Mau are out there
in their villages right now, or hiding.
Would you all care to join me
in going after these fucking apes.
There are guns for everybody.

Monty Parker stood up, clapped.
Right. I want to bag me a brace
of these awful niggers.

Prior stood up,
checking his pockets.

Tom's eyes met his father's.
I ought to go back,
for Kate and your mother.
Can't leave them undefended
with this going on.

Of course.

But you should go, Tom.
You'll be useful. And it's time,
I'm afraid, you know,
to be a man and all that.

Jenkins was beside them: *Well?*

Get one for me, Tom.
So Tom's father offered Tom,
offered him up
with an awkward shove
as men offer their sons
out into the world.

I'm heading back to ours.
My wife and daughter.
Tom's all for it, though.

Good, good. Prior will sort you out.

*

Equipped, going, in an open-
backed vehicle, with torch and gun
and whistle, gripping the metal frame
as stars tossed and righted themselves,
the vehicle flounced and skittered
down the terrible road,
Tom felt awfully close to laughing.
His chest seethed with it.
All these men, armed,

some still in their bow-ties,
grave-faced, could they mean it?
The whole thing was ludicrous:
the boy-scout planning, the boxes of ammo.
Prior sat forwards, holding the muzzle
of his rifle with both hands,
riding easily, without seeming to notice
the sudden wincing drops and sickening floats.

Out of the vehicles. Into the stillness
of a night of loud insects.
Cooling engines ticked.
Hysteria subsided: they *were* serious.
And the night's soft, huge darkness approached,
breathed up behind them,
shaping for murder. Tom felt it touch
the back of his head. In the twisting
torch lights they made decisions.
Tom was assigned to two Home Guards
whose names he didn't catch
and his throat closed when he tried to ask,
his inner surfaces clamping.
They would roam for hideaways
away from the villages.
Others would start at the villages
and clean them out.

*

Began for Tom a difficult walk.
He felt weightless with fear
but hurt with effort – these men
walked fast – and black shapes
sometimes hit him, branches.
He felt, he really felt,
the trajectory from the end of his gun,
a line, a beam, projecting
hundreds of yards, loose,
swinging as he walked,

slicing through, and all along
that line whenever he wanted it, death.

*

Prior saw her, the pretty cropped head,
the high breasts, the wide frightened eyes,
and grabbed her by the forearm,
the decision made in his body
before he had thought:
to leave the men and their business,
to grab and vanish with her.
He pulled her arm, starting to run.
Quick, girl. Very dangerous here.
Come on. Safer. Safer!

*

Everything flocking into darkness.
Tom had to keep after them to see.
Glimpses flared, were lost,
kept plunging out of sight,
if they were glimpses.
His weightless legs bumped under him,
cringed at distant gunfire.
His two men stopped.
There, pointing at the richer, feathered black of undergrowth.
When I say. Tom raised his gun.
Now. And all fired.
Tom saw his extended arm in flashes
as the shots went off.
A voice in his head counted the bangs,
totalled seven between them.
Cease fire! They walked to the spot.
One Home Guard nudged the body with his foot.
Tom looked, then up at the lurching trees.
It had looked just like a man.
The way the fingers curled.
You got your first, sir.
Tom tucked his hot gun

into his waistband to be able
to shake their hands.

*

The place Prior found was so dark
that he could hardly see her:
a flex of mauve on her skin,
the white corners of her eyes.
Certainly no one would hear them,
much less care, what with the shrieks and gunfire.
She gave him no trouble to speak of.
After one good slap that salted her mouth
she was compliant, only
repeating some phrase over
and over, like a bird's stupid song.
But he was right, he was right
to take her. Face down,
with a little forcing – her phrase getting faster –
he was in, pushing, pushing,
her buttocks greasy, cold against his belly,
her little breaths shunted out
in time to him, her warm, elegant
neck in his right hand,
her left bicep in his left,
her dry hole burning him.
Breezes lifted the sweat from him.
After his narrow, painful release,
No harm done. Good girl,
he lit a cigarette then helped her up
and, smoking, watched her run away.

*

Why had Tom thought they'd stop
after the first kill, as though they'd done enough?
Of course they didn't.
Over the long night they killed two more,
a modest tally by others' standards.
The second one Tom didn't shoot.

He held his gun up while the others shot
and watched him fall.
The third came after long hours,
with splintery light through the trees.
By now, trekking back,
they could smell the burning villages everywhere.
Tom's legs itched horribly.
His shirt sucked at his skin,
rubbed a slow burn into his collar.
There were bodies everywhere
in different attitudes:
stunned, reaching, sleeping, tumbled.
Then from behind something a man sprang up
and Tom shot him.
Just like in a Western: the attacking Indian:
Tom saw the man look straight at him,
clownish with terror
as he pulled the trigger,
saw the bullet make a splash
in the man's bare chest.
Only the fall backwards was different,
looser and ugly, spastic, almost embarrassing.
A Home Guard walked up sideways,
slowly, and shot again the wriggling man.

                    *

Back at the vehicles, the men murmured,
passing round a hip-flask.
The sky was oppressively bright,
acres of weightless gold above them.
Prior saw Tom's face
and walked over to him,
placed his hand on Tom's shoulder.
You'll be all right, old man.
Chipper after some sleep.
First time is always the worst.
Tom turned, unable … to thank,
and held on to his wrist.

John Fuller

I sat on Beatrix Lehmann's knee, terrified that she was
      undead;

I saw Laurel and Hardy alive at the Lewisham Hippodrome,
      and they were gratified by my laughter;

I bowed to Queen Mary, widow of George V, in Greenwich
      Park, and from her limousine of midnight hue she
      nodded graciously back;

I was inspected in full uniform by Field-Marshal Montgomery:
      his cornflower-blue eyes passed within twenty inches
      of mine, and he departed in a bullet-proof car;

I sang for Vaughan Williams, his great head sunk on his
      waistcoat, neither awake nor asleep;

I watched Jonathan Miller lift a white mouse by its tail and
      drop it in a killing-bottle for me as an illustration of
      something or other;

I saw Frank Swift pick up a football with one hand;

I waited in the wings for my own entrance while Oliver
      Sacks played de Falla's 'Ritual Fire Dance' in a sash
      and a lurid spotlight;

I asked T. S. Eliot what he was writing, and his answer shall
      remain a secret;

I rang up the curtain on Dennis Potter in his first public
      performance, playing the part of a Romanian-French
      playwright;

I trod the throbbing boards of an ocean liner with Burt
      Lancaster, who was very small, and who smiled his
      characteristically delicate sneering smile;

I was asked to stay on in my first job, but politely declined
      and was succeeded in office by the Earl of Gowrie;

I drove Edward Albee to Niagara Falls, where he was silent
      among the thickly-iced trees;

I held Sam Mendes in my arms, but was more interested in
      his father's collection of Japanese pornography;

I brushed away cobwebs that had been sprayed on my hair
      by David Attenborough;

I played heads-bodies-and-legs with Henry Moore;

The Poet Laureate sent me reams of his verse, which I
      regretfully refused to publish;

I handed Debra Winger a glass of wine and did not tell her
      who I was;

I played against William Golding's French Defence and
      infiltrated my King's Knight to d6 and he couldn't
      avoid going a piece down;

And all this is true, and life is but a trail of dust between the
      stars;

The unremembered shall be forgotten, and the remembered
      also;

The dead shall be dead, and also the living.

Sam Gardiner

BRAVE FACE

Wednesday being the longest day, here comes
Major Heartburn Bomb-tick Bickerstaff,
eggshell skull bobbing across the car park
in broken sunshine. He wrestles the door
to a standstill and looks round in terrible triumph.
The security camera slowly averts its gaze.
When the Ice Age was cracking up
and landscaping the county like a golf course
it fashioned a drumlin of boulder clay
where a future major would be taught to shoot
unarmed rabbits, as he confesses to his dogs.
When he returned he found no trace of himself.
His drumlin was being brought low for shops
and cars and, the dogs were dismayed to learn,
the last rabbits in their bunkers were being
mopped up by sappers in bloody buggies,
tyres treading huge caterpillars into the mud.
The air in the Mortality Clinic is thin with altitude,
too thin for all but a toothy whistling of old hits
and ancient jaws cracking 'Long time no sea,
as the gulls remarked of the limestone uplands,'
where fish lie gasping among waves of grass.
The entrenched warrior hands us his pain and says,
'Feel that.' He shares his anticoagulant with the rats
because good health is abnormal, an abnegation
of reality, a leaping of the chasm that opens wider
with each season of longjohns and flu jabs.
One man's meat. Quips and cranks. Please miss.
Ma'moiselle! Another man's poisson! Never
a teardrop whatever, for one is all that's needed
to start a river, send it collecting tributaries,
bursting banks to become a flood,
rivering into basements, ruining the carpets,

carpeting the ruins. Cheerio! Back to the front!
And off he hobbles, perhaps to a silent barracks
whose stately walls are panelled with stilled lifes,
repros of Cellini, Caravaggio and the mob,
and old bitches hung as lamb who smile villainously
down at straightbacked books ranked shoulder
to shoulder in jackets of dust, and a roll-top desk
at which a fake Hepplewhite chair wears his blazer.
The trouble with old men, he tells the red setters,
is old women who leave their voices to brattle
about the house in the morning, and again at dusk.
And the dogs, listening attentively for variations
in the old soliloquy, subside into the hairy ginger carpet
and, from under tented brows, watch the skeletons
begin to dance on the platforms of his epaulettes.

Deborah Garrison

I Saw You Walking

I saw you walking in Newark Penn Station
in your shoes of white ash. At the corner
of my nervous glance your dazed passage
first forced me away, tracing the crescent
berth you'd give a drunk, a lurcher, nuzzling
all comers with ill will and his stench, but
not this one, not today: one shirt arm's sheared
clean from the shoulder, the whole bare limb
wet with muscle and shining dimly pink,
the other full-sheathed in cotton, Brooks Bros
type, the cuff yet buttoned at the wrist, a
parody of careful dress, preparedness –
so you had not rolled up your sleeves yet this
morning when your suit jacket (here are
the pants, dark gray, with subtle stripe, as worn
by men like you on ordinary days)
and briefcase (you've none, reverse commuter
come from the pit with nothing to carry
but your life) were torn from you, as your life
was not. Your face itself seemed to be walking,
leading your body north, though the age
of the face, blank and ashen, passing forth
and away from me, was unclear, the sandy
crown of hair powdered white like your feet, but
underneath not yet gray – forty-seven?
forty-eight? the age of someone's father –
and I trembled for your luck, for your broad
dusted back, half shirted, walking away;
I should have dropped to my knees to thank God
you were alive, O my God, in whom I don't believe.

Lavinia Greenlaw

Maeshowe

The year's low country.
Sun rolls, sky rises and is long gone.

Not to see the framing steepness
you lower your head.

You are line.
A form of utterance from last to next

no more than murmur
as light pulls into the seed of itself

a held breath
your body, an earthbound chamber.

Why rush past into whiteness?

This is the birth of the dark half
the serpent days of seem.

Scribbles of lust and brag
speak like needles on the skin.

Fal Estuary

The night train's chain of events.
What could be brighter?
Window by window

shocking and invisibly connected
as if we travel on our nerves.
At the end of the line

a milky geography of salt and chalk
seaweed caught in the arms of an oak
a high streaming field

where a hare starts out of the earth
wheels like a girl woken and told
to surface. *Now?* Now.

The hare, the girl
break up into a dance
of unready yellows and greens.

Blakeney Point

Such constancy is no celebration.
Under such careful light
it is only earth we walk on.

The long day empties.
The small things, so vital, quicken and fly.
Already no song in the garden.

The fires we build along the northern edge
are no more upsetting to the air
than breath. Is this love?

A cure for the visible.
Fern seed gathered this midsummer midnight
would render us as clear.

Severn

When the weather comes always and sideways
it's not enough, the settling. Why is this known
only and over as first and not all over again?

Each time the tide overtakes itself
what's worked loose is moved inland on river
over-running river taking with it all the warm shades
the tree-chimney-telegraph wreckage of your way home.

It starts with a lapse, a taking back
of background, breeze and creep and song
a making room for the massive collapse of distance
the roll of the world into a wave that will not break

and does not break until the world is moved inland
to break down the door of a house where a man
turns in his sleep and reaches past his wife for his lover
his lover for his wife, setting fire to his hair.

Paul Groves

AGAINST STEREOTYPE

Two fitters install a kitchen in our suburban home:
twentysomething, muscular, earringed, jaunty…
yet their ghettoblaster plays Grieg. I note a scattering
of other CDs – Albinoni, Fauré, Orff – and double take
at their vocabulary: Craig uses 'juxtaposition',
Jason 'totemic'. Only then do their movements register:
rarefied, balletic, though not mincing or effeminate.
Craig holds his screwdriver with the sensitivity
of a portraitist; Jason plies his mallet with the precision
of a Christie's auctioneer. I sigh as Peer Gynt
fills the room, and crane to discover whether it is,
as suspected, Karajan who wields the baton.
My admiration peaks when they break for lunch:
no white bread sandwiches, crisps, chocolate bars,
but salade niçoise, Gruyère, iced coffee soufflés.
They knock off punctiliously at five, exiting
with a Restoration flourish. The room is depleted
by their passing, the house palpably colder.
The cul-de-sac withers as their van leaves it.

Kelly Grovier

Camping Out

The infinite regression of things
was never made clearer to you
than that starless night
when you took the form
of a chattering chicken's head
projected onto the nylon
wall of a tent, and looking back

at the pinched forefinger and thumb
that made your beak, back
through the clenched middle and ring
fingers to the flickering
kerosene lantern, you knew that even he,
your pudgy, rotten-toothed, dim-
witted creator, could not behold what

you, a knuckle-brained silhouette
could see on the other side
of the screen: the racoon at the picnic
basket, the speckled fawn disappearing
under brush for fear, and beyond
the timberline, the fat orange moon
that was busy, obliterating the stars.

Paul Henry

THE BLACK GUITAR

Clearing out ten years from a wardrobe
I opened its lid and saw *Joe*
written twice in its dust, in a child's hand,
then a squiggled seagull or two.

                              Joe, Joe
a man's tears are worth nothing,
but a child's name in the dust, or in the sand
of a darkening beach, that's a life's work.

I touched two strings, to hear how much
two lives can slip out of tune

                              then I left it,
brought down the night on it, for fear, Joe
of hearing your unbroken voice, or the sea
if I played it.

Kevin Higgins

MY MILITANT TENDENCY

It's nineteen eighty two and I know everything.
Hippies are people who always end up asking
Charles Manson to sing them another song.
I'd rather be off putting some fascist through
a glass door arseways, but being fifteen,
have to mow the lawn first. Last year,

Liverpool meant football; now
it's the Petrograd of the British Revolution.
Instead of masturbation, I find socialism.
While others dream of businessmen bleeding
in basements; I promise to abolish double-chemistry class
the minute I become Commissar. In all of this
there is usually a leather jacket involved. I tell

cousin Walter and his lovely new wife, Elizabeth,
to put their aspirations in their underpants
and smoke them; watch

my dad's life become a play:
Sit Down in Anger.

Peter Howard

THE USES OF MOWN GRASS

Once we've heard the sleepy rattle of the cutters,
we're a class of children in a summer classroom,
but our minds have already all run out
to the field beyond the playground,

so there's no point, Miss, in trying to keep
our attention on adding up and taking away,
leaving a finger space, or Janet and John:
we're busy making our plans for later.

Some of us will mark out the rooms of houses:
neat lines of cuttings, with a gap for a window,
another for the front door,
so we can invite the neighbours in for tea.

Some will make ocean liners, or space rockets;
and argue incessantly about the design,
which has most room, or goes fastest
and whether Darrell Bowser should be allowed on board.

Others will pile it up like miser's gold.
Never satisfied with what they collect themselves,
they'll pinch your kitchen wall, or mast, or booster,
if you don't keep an eye out for them.

It's warmer than snow, more fragrant,
but it doesn't stick together as well:
so the air, when the battle starts,
will be thick with green confetti.

There will be squadrons of aeroplanes,
a green fragmentation bomb in each outstretched fist.
And there will be one who stuffs it down the back
of Julie Parfitt's dress, mixed with nettles.

Katia Kapovich

The Girl That Saved a Village

The animals knew everything.
On the morning before the tsunami
the girl's cat carried her kittens out
and led them up the hill;
the cows abandoned their pasture
and roamed further inland;
some goats quarreled at first
for the position of the leader,
but soon enough trotted away through the woods
like a defeated army;
pigs, big skeptics in the face of change,
became disquieted and left the village
in an organized crowd followed
by the deaf village shepherd.

As she came home from school
and her parents told her
that the water had withdrawn far away from the shore,
she also knew what it meant.
Predictably, they didn't want to believe her;
how could she know if
she was only ten years old,
and her geography book could be wrong anyway.
So she ran to the beach
where people were rummaging
through the sandy wasteland
picking crabs and fish.
The bottom of the ocean lay naked and breathless
like a woman after delivering a baby.
There, she stripped off her school uniform
and screamed until they couldn't ignore her anymore;

'Big wave is coming! Big wave is coming!'

Mimi Khalvati

IMPENDING WHITENESS

i
It was only in retrospect we knew
it was coming. We weren't thinking in colour,
we were thinking in animal, a new
category of thought and feeling. Dull
as the plates of encyclopedias are,
they were imprinted on our memories.
Comparison was called for and erasure,
and greeting the continents' emissaries:

Bennett's wallaby, Reeves' muntjac, red marmot,
Chinese water deer (solitary things),
mara and peafowl by the dozen roaming
freely through the carparks and café, spotted
from the steam train and waved to, then forgotten
underfoot, so fickle are human beings.

ii
It was only in retrospect we knew
how close we were to birth and to the spirit.
Whiteness came as a chick. At first it grew
as a question without our asking it.
Why is it white? we wondered, staring at mud
and the cesspool where the black rhino pissed,
is it male? Does the peacock's tail that floods
more colour than we can bear grow out of this?

We didn't ask, entranced by size and scale
as we were and the picture of a peahen
ushering two plain daughters and the male
heir to her husband's looks into a pen
where the poor rhino, never one to threaten
small children, backed off as they strode in gaily.

iii
It was only in retrospect we knew
how a paintbrush slides from the zebra's flank
down to the shin; how it drops from the blue
to swirl in the depths of a mottled tank
three layers of dapple: cloud, water, seal.
How often have we thought, looking at art,
what is that creature, mythical or real?
Equally, seeing life imitate art,

marvelled at evolution's artifice.
But if the model were extinct, as this
white donkey from north Iran almost is,
we would never have found in Bedfordshire,
from the heart of a Persian miniature,
a half-horse, half-mule, we thought legendary.

iv
It was only in retrospect we knew
white animals, like stones, had laid a trail
behind us: runes from which we might construe
something magical, lodestars that would pale
into nothing. Weather was part of it,
light weakening. And the end of the summer.
And distance, too, that made white tusks hit us
in the eye but the bull elephant dimmer,

a pierced surround for butts of ivory.
The strange became familiar and domestic
cows, ponies, grazing with camels, exotic.
White rhino, no more white than the black are black,
walled a line of oaks an – Rabbit! a cry
shot out while yak announced prehistory.

v
It was only in retrospect we knew,
passing a pygmy goat so white it shone

like a ghost and the silence fell, wind blew
and the trees and grass, with everyone gone,
came into their own, that this place never closed.
We could come in the dark by moonlight, torchlight,
recapture, in the smell of dung that rose
like a flood in the dusk, worlds without sight.

We would be the ones at a disadvantage,
seen but not seeing. We would be as men
and the animals behind bars veiled women,
watching. Matriarchs cornered in a cage,
waiting, waiting for the patriarch's rage.
We would be perpetrators, if and when.

vi
It was only in retrospect we knew
it broke our hearts to hear the howling, see them
moving, an older cub among them, and through
the wire fencing, feel the desire to be them,
like them, even the lone wolf wandering,
nose to the ground, in the wood. They seemed at home,
content to congregate on the hill with nothing
to call them further afield, nowhere to roam.

In this country, they died out long ago.
But past the wolf wood, in an open meadow
that took us by surprise as if our worst fears
seen in broad daylight or here, by the glow
of a moon, really were to disappear,
white wolves have lived among us all these years.

vii
It was only in retrospect we knew
it was whiteness everything heads toward.
None of the animals minded us; few
held our gaze but with a tacit accord,
as though we too had a natural place

in the scheme of things, as indeed we had,
allowed us to observe them. But the grace
of lowered necks, lofty horns and ears glad

to obey command words more readily
than children, created an aching barrier,
an invisible veil nothing could tear.
As we headed for the car, solitary
in the carpark, a safari bus roared by
with a bride, waving, throned in the open air.

Whipsnade Wild Animal Park

John Kinsella

COLOURS OF THE WHEATBELT

If all colours therein are to be found in the spectral tail-feathers
of a 28 parrot, so are they to be found in the flickering slither
of a juvenile dugite, come into the house through an uncovered
drainpipe, working the polish of the stone-tiled floor
hard for traction, and sending shudders through the air
like a photo taken out of focus so that resonances
of the body shape unfold like an incremental halo
about its form – intentionally. In the half-light
of the corridor the translucent then opaque
olive green gives way to an under-shadow
of night-rich blackness, the ochre of its adult
manifestation a slippage between the overlap of scales,
a body stretching beneath the set weight of its skin,
a place to shelter searched out, senses hard pressed
and the thin darkness of narrow places
a rainbow dense with chemical light
of its touch, the streaming colours within.

James Liddy

Preamble.
I saw only the naked high priest
in the dead flower of bread
behind the glass.

I read in the pension
'Ode To The Most Holy Sacrament of the Altar.'
The hands open like flower to receive
every time I do that I remember the heavy curtain
between this world and the next
the ray drifting down the galleries
so happy with light mouth
towards the fairy in glory.

Cornered in white pants white tie
against the sloping white-washed cottages
from door to door to collect First Communion boxes
pockets bright with de Valera shillings,
wandering over the stone bridge's arch
to the landlord's Masonic trees
standing everywhere for the pure photograph.

Brides.
The priest passes into the bride
'Faith of our mothers holy faith.'

Ian, Casey, and I
drive the encroached-on vega
past the Duke of Wellington's poplars.

Oranges are beautiful
that means poems may hang on their trees
but sometimes they might be lemons

will God eat the oranges
on the tree in Lorca's yard?
The tree waving in its manger.

(People wear earrings,
how far did Franco restrict the Carnival?
Ian doesn't hear my question.)

Tree branches speak poems
in fairy tales, is more eaten?

Ahora Lorca
a cot
a photograph
bestowed by a sister.
Formal poems of kissing on the walls
and on the leaves outside,
wreaths
inside words.

Fairies may have provided the cot
and they certainly like wars,
the best wars are between museums
the Huerta de San Vicente against this one.
This glass case has quests
the Huerta glass has questions:
can a man kissing a man be a love poet,
can a homosexual who writes passionate letters be passionate,
male lovers are singers in their own Operas?

Another poet of Granada in charge of
photos postcards proofs upstairs,

Juan de Loxa whispers with a cold
opening a package from Cuba.

I should explain Casey and I were looking
for the Spicer/Lorca correspondence
which is hidden somewhere
within a radius of 20 kilometers
or has it been set alight under a tree
or buried so deeply in the vega
that they are for ever secret letters?

On a video upstairs someone who knew the poet
is talking to a group of women.
Ian says, 'Lorca wrote passionate letters
to this man but he's too embarrassed to use them.'

Let poems hang on letter trees
murmuring words
to receive words back.

We drive back to the city
Federico is up on the bar wall
Ian's biography lies on a shelf.

On the street friends left
only the family went up the hill
with the bodies.
On the Paseo de Los Tristes
spill your guts.

Anna McKerrow

OCCASIONAL LOVER

I know you know I'm looking.
You can feel my look, ripping
your top buttons off, my thumb in your mouth;
latitude and languorous plans are not ours,
we live minutes hand to mouth;
no breadth, no depth: no flow,
more a colliding of power –
and it's just some of you, no time for all, just some,
and that time is rushed and rough;
but you're enough, occasional lover; enough.

Richard Marggraf Turley

ANNING

Months after I bury my father,
I dig up a monster. It rises
snapping from the marl
like a crocodile, one vast eye
fixed on the trowel.

So there's the cabinet-maker
again, fussing over my puzzle-
work, its interlocking parts.
I think of nothing to say,
give myself to the fish-lizards.

Valeria Melchioretto

THE TEAR PERCOLATOR

From the kitchen window I could see the locomotive
rip through the swollen and inflamed backdrop.
I was kneeling on a stool almost as tall as myself,
leaning right out into the open, late summer air,
resting my head like a Raphael angel.

Indoors the espresso hissed, spitting black drops.
Steam blurred the vision, questions always drowned
in suppressed air…

My father wore a thin coat of lead under his skin.
He cried on occasions, percolated tears from behind
the retina. The crying gene was built in like an oil pump,
responsible for cooling his worn system.

Our grey Sunday outings: the newsagent's by the station.
The factory ground on the way back was full of
ship-engine-embryos and train-skeletons.
I looked into his cloudy face, a taste of metal on my tongue.

Matt Merritt

HOLIDAY, 1939

When it heaved up from the sea loch
with its whaleback glistening
to bask under Indian
summer sun, us all listening

for the first grumble or roar
that would hurtle us headlong,
scrambling for the bikes, it was
the minister's straight-backed son

who identified it
as a modified Class VII,
workhorse of the Kriegsmarine,
but it was Callum McCallum,

tenth of that name, who stepped
forward and commanded it
back to the grey depths.
Rock doves wheezed above us

all the way home, and so
it slipped beneath, below,
back out into the narrows,
a legendary beast, unknown to God.

David Morley

BEARS

for Gabriel John Keenan Morley

PawPaw and Paprika, two great bears of the Egyptians
of Lancashire, the Witches' County, Chohawniskey Tem

who, when our camp plucked its tents and pulled out its maps,
walked steadily with the wagons, ambling, always ambling,

all across the open pages of wet England, footing
as far as Pappin-eskey Tem, the flat Duck County,

crossing to Curo-mengreskey Gav, the Boxers' Town;
padded on to Paub-pawnugo Tem, Apple-Water County

as good for bears as for their Gypsy masters, although
who is master is moot after much apple-water;

then to bide by Bokra-mengreskey Tem, Shepherds' County,
for their collies are trained not to bark at bears, but slyly, gently,

slink big-eyed as children behind their shepherd's greeting.

Ambling, bears, always ambling... mooching to Mi-develeskey Tem,
My God's Town, the God for all bears too,

God of paws and padding, of Polar, Kodiak and Koala;
sniffing superiorly through Dinelo Tem, the Fools' County;

circling with our circus to Shammin-engreskey Gav, Chairmakers'
Town,
nosing north through Lil-engreskey Gav, a Town Made of Readers,

then paws over eyes for Kaulo Gav, the Black Town;
joy at Jinney-mengreskey Gav, the Sharpers' Town;

to Lancashire as it was then, wider county of white witches,
to the clean camps, to the great brown bears of the Egyptians.

To PawPaw and Paprika, backwards in time they go, pad pad.
Goodbye.

The bears' route: Lancashire to Lincolnshire to Nottingham to
Herefordshire to Sussex to Canterbury *through* Suffolk to Windsor
through Oxford to Birmingham to Manchester and Lancashire.

Julie O'Callaghan

Lettergesh Strand

has all these ghosts
running through the
windy spray.
Wave after wave
of people I know
haunting the beach
like translucent jellyfish.
There goes my father
examining a rock pool
with a starfish floating.
I wish a handful of bleached sand
didn't remind me of that
plastic bag labelled
*This package contains
the cremated remains of…*

*

The ringing
gets louder.
I search everywhere:
I push aside soft
rounded rocks,
globs of seaweed,
pick up a tiny
curved shell
and hold it
to my ear.
Your voice
– a little distant –
is talking to me,
telling your old jokes,
gushing about

where you are now.
It's great to hear
from you.

I should have known
you'd be hanging out
on this chilly Connemara beach.
No – I'm not in a rush.
Keep talking.
I'm listening.

Ciaran O'Driscoll

PLEASE HOLD

This is the future, my wife says.
We are already there, and it's the same
as the present. Your future, here, she says.
And I'm talking to a robot on the phone.
The robot is giving me countless options,
none of which answer to my needs.
Wonderful, says the robot
when I give him my telephone number.
And *Great*, says the robot
when I give him my account number.
I have a wonderful telephone number
and a great account number,
but I can find nothing to meet my needs
on the telephone, and into my account
(which is really the robot's account)
goes money, *my* money, to pay for nothing.
I'm paying a robot for doing nothing.
This call is free of charge, says the mind-reading robot.
Yes but I'm paying for it, I shout,
out of my wonderful account
into my great telephone bill.
Wonderful, says the robot.
And my wife says, This is the future.
I'm sorry, I don't understand, says the robot.
Please say Yes or No.
Or you can say Repeat or Menu.
You can say Yes, No, Repeat or Menu,
Or you can say Agent if you'd like to talk
to someone real, who is just as robotic.
I scream Agent! and am cut off,
and my wife says, This is the future.
We are already there and it's the same
as the present. Your future, here, she says.

And I'm talking to a robot on the phone,
and he is giving me no options
in the guise of countless alternatives.
We appreciate your patience. Please hold.
Eine Kleine Nachtmusik. Please hold.
Eine Kleine Nachtmusik. Please hold.
Eine fucking Kleine Nachtmusik.
And the robot transfers me to himself.
Your call is important to us, he says.
And my translator says, This means
your call is not important to them.
And my wife says, This is the future.
And my translator says, Please hold
means that, for all your accomplishments,
the only way you can now meet your needs
is by looting. *Wonderful*, says the robot

Please hold. Please grow old. Please grow cold.
Please do what you're told. Grow old. Grow cold.
This is the future. Please hold.

Niall O'Sullivan

The Father in Law

He came with the missus, part of the package.
He brought his old chair. His wife's ashes.
He sat there all day, never talking,
not to me or his daughter.
Not to admonish the toddlers
when they threw milk at his trousers.
Not a groan when the dog chewed his toes.
He only opened his mouth to shovel in food
which he chewed slowly, miserably.

He was always the last to leave the living room,
I'd pretend to be interested in Newsnight
hoping he'd go to bed before
they showed those arty films.
Never happened, and when I rose
in the early hours to cut my sandwiches
and head off to the thankless job,
he was there, sat still, scantly lit.
That was when I heard the breathing most;
Innocent particles of oxygen
sucked into the darkest place on earth,
then released, corrupted, polluting the air.
Alone with him, I'd shout
obscenities into his face, did terrible
things to his wife's ashes as he looked on.
Of course, the missus wouldn't put him in a home.
I started thinking that come the day he died,
she'd have him stuffed and sat back on that chair.

The only way that I could get my life back
was if I could make him scream, jump, even twitch.
So I bought a gun from a Polish mate at work,
took it home, stood in front of him, took aim.

Shot the old sod's left ear clean off.
Not a scream, not a jolt, not a bead of sweat
just the smell of hot blood, pouring,
not a tear as I pushed the muzzle into his forehead
not a smile to show that finally, he'd won.

I've heard of men in India that sit
unmoved for years, no food or water,
they do so through some peace they've found within,
but that was never the case with him.
It was some old hatred that kept him going,
something terrible that he would never forgive,
a cold rhythm, fierce quiet where his heart once was.

Alice Oswald

Two Moon Poems

1 In a Tidal Valley

flat stone sometimes lit sometimes not
one among many moodswung creatures
that have settled in this beautiful
Uncountry of an Estuary

swans pitching your wings
in the reedy layby of a vacancy
where the house of the sea
can be set up quickly and taken down in an hour

all you flooded and stranded weeds whose workplace
is both a barren mud-site and a speeded up garden
full of lake-offerings and slabs of light
which then unwills itself listen

all you crabs in the dark alleys of the wall
all you mudswarms ranging up and down
I notice you are very alert and worn out
skulking about and grabbing what you can

listen this is not the ordinary surface river
this is not river at all this is something
like a huge repeating mechanism
banging and banging the jetty

very hard to define, most close in kind
to the mighty angels of purgatory
who come solar-powered into darkness
using no other sails than their shining wings

yes this is the Moon this hurrying
muscular unsolid unstillness
this endless wavering in whose engine
I too am living

2 Mud

this evening those very thin fence posts
struggled up out of the mud again
and immediately the meal began, there was
that flutter of white napkins of waders hurrying in

there was that bent old egret
prodding and poising his knife and fork
and so many mucous mudglands
so much soft throat sucking at my feet

I thought be careful this is deep mud this is
pure mouth it has such lip muscles
such a suction of wet kisses
the slightest contact clingfilms your hands

there goes that dunlin up to her chin in
the simmering dish of mush and
all night that seeping feeding sound
of moistness digesting smallness

and then I creep-slid out over the grey weed,
and all those slimy foodpods burst under me
I thought I know whose tongue I'm
treading on and under whose closed eye

every stone every shell every sock
every bone will be crammed in.
to my unease the meal went on and on
there were those queues of reeds

dipping their straws in the dead
there was that sly tide swiftly refilling
I thought really I should have webbed feet
I should have white wings to walk here

Victoria Pugh

All That Glisters

The escalators pour down from the first floor,
and splash in the glass bowl of the entrance hall.

Shoppers step on, and glide down the silver stairs,
a stream of queens, or ancient popes on rollers.

Jerseys in packets are colour cards in secret corners,
navy for town, green and purple on the grouse moor.

Buckles, black patent handbags, buttons and cutlery,
flicker out their message – 'Buy me, I'm shiny.'

Gold make-up on lit-up counters – polish and pearl,
bronzing and blusher – 'You too can be beautiful.'

Through the doors to the caff in the staff quarters.
Stale coke drips from seats and sticks to the walls.

Men ogle the new girl and like the size of her tits.
Women say, 'I hate my boss, she's such a bitch.'

Ladies put away cardigans and pairs of smelly shoes;
and then they slam their locker doors as they go.

Angela Readman

Housewife

She will make herself pretty before you come home,
spray scent on her wrists, a reflex mist between her breasts.

You will walk into the kitchen.
Everything will be pristine.
The reflection of your hands on her chest
in stainless steel like a hall of mirrors.
You will swirl your keys on one finger.
Keys and fobs she notices multiply each year,
the way you clank them down next to her
as if their weight should tell her something.

She will get drunk on your breath,
mixed with the scent of Fairy that's kind to her hands.
You will kiss her as if she is a stranger.
She will wonder what you have seen
that makes you act this way today.

You will drink black coffee,
taken with a little sugar these days.
She wipes cupboard doors clean of the smears of fingers
and starts on the meal, tidies whoever she was away.

Robin Robertson

By Clachan Bridge
for Alasdair Roberts

I remember the girl
with the hare-lip
down by Clachan Bridge,
cutting up fish
to see how they worked;
by morning's end her nails
were black red, her hands
all sequined silver.
She simplified rabbits
to a rickle of bones;
dipped into a dormouse
for the pip of its heart.
She'd open everything,
that girl.
They say they found
wax dolls in her wall,
poppets full of human hair,
but I'd say they're wrong.
What's true is
that the blacksmith's son,
the simpleton,
came down here once,
fathomed her, and bucked.
Claimed she licked him
clean as a whistle.
I remember the tiny stars
of her hands around her belly
as it grew and grew, and how
after a year, nothing came.
How she said it was still there,
inside her, a stone-baby.
And how I saw her wrists

blue-bangled with scars
and those hands flittering
at her throat,
to the plectrum of bone
she'd hung there.
As to what happened
to the blacksmith's boy,
no one knows
and I'll keep my tongue.
Last thing I heard, the starlings
had started
to mimic her crying,
and she'd learned how to fly.

Stephen Romer

MAGISTRATE

At the end he sat bolt upright
and read the riot act
to an empty ward:

hooligans and vandals
came back to haunt
his closing statement.

Carol Rumens

CLOTHES LEFT ON A WASHING-LINE
in the Gaza Strip, 2005

What could we do, when the Jews came for the Jews
to tell them there is no God,
there are no miracles?

We hung, collars down, in the usual manner,
motionless in the sun, our dyes blazing
like the peonies and jacaranda
planted all round us by our clever weavers
as they went on giving God the credit for everything –
the desert, the city, even the rotary clothes-line.
We hung together, helpless when their fury
shook us like an unfamiliar wind.
They howled they were coming back, they were going to feed us
again their hard strong lives, their strenuous occupation.
We, who had shielded their bodies,
couldn't cover up this stupidity.
Forgive us, but we're clothes, not flags: we're realists.

And when the Palestinians come
to tear us from our pegs and make a bonfire,
happy that we're so shallow and boneless and wicked,
we'll tell them exactly what the Jews told the Jews:
there is no God, there are no miracles.

Lorna Shaughnessy

Grasping the Nettle

Nothing stings the memory like nettles.
I squeeze the sap from a dock leaf onto a small hand
and recall a girl who tried to jump a stream, stumbled,
clutching wildly at the first solid-looking clump of green,
not pausing to measure stream, leg or consequence
and the shocked revelation of pain
that screamed from hand to brain.

She entered the street stage right, hand held aloft
like a messenger from the battlefield.
Her uncle shook his head and held the hand
beneath a tap outside the byre.

And it was hard to tell which gave the sharper sting,
the blisters rising on her palm, the icy shock of water,
or the salty taste of shame on her lips.

Jean Sprackland

Mattresses

Tipped down the embankment, they
sprawl like sloshed suburban wives,

buckled and split, slashed by rain,
moulded by bodies dead or disappeared
and reeking with secrets.

A lineside museum of sleep and sex,
an archive of thrills and emissions,
the histories of half-lives
spent hiding in the dark.

Arthritic iron frames might still be worth a bit,
but never that pink quilted headboard,
naked among thistles, relic
of some reckless beginning, testament

to the usual miracle: the need to be close,
whatever the stains or the bruises.

Greta Stoddart

WANT

in the voice if an unconceived child

The more you look the more remote
I am to you not as a star but a stone

kicked to the edge of a lane two roads in
from the sea in a dead-end town.

You won't think to look there
because you're here

in this bright room, bent over the blur
of threads that's led you here where

you daren't move for fear of upsetting
whatever it is that's stopping you getting

what you want – a tower
of fine bone china

in a dark corner,
growing higher and higher;

here where you come closest to me,
me who is really you – you

as small, knuckled want,
impotent, clean, clock-watching want.

But you know how it is.
I'll come to you when you're a mess,

pissed probably, putting it about,
when you've loosed yourself from the thought

of yourself and world crashes in with its crowds
of stricken infants, its mad array of flowers.

O oestrogen, astrology, buseralin and cells,
HCG, Day 14, the transmigration of souls!

It's all more than you could ever know.
So stop, little no-mother, come and throw

yourself back onto a strong wind –
take in the sky, hold on to nothing.

Maggie Sullivan

An Everyday Epic

A toddler,
a baby,
four bags of shopping,
a hill,
then a wheel falls off the pram.

The children are in conspiracy today –
it's a nappy marathon
but the washing machine
is still in the repair shop.

She is in the garden
burying shopping, pram wheel,
nappies and washing machine
as deep

as she can,
tucks the children up in their beds.
They sense her mulch of rage and tenderness.

Michael Symmons Roberts

Origin of Species

So, this is the root of us, this browning
bed of bracken, palm leaves, feathers,

in the cool lee of a once great tree.
Here, Adam and Eve began one night

the chinese whispers of genetics.
One sultry night perhaps, or maybe one

so cold they held each other tight
beneath the leaves for warmth.

Now – in its fall – the tree is gold
and amber, and has shed its countless

chestnuts, pursed and glistening.
On this bed of spikes two blind white

mink are sleeping, curled into a catherine
wheel. There is nothing here to mark

this as the place where humankind began,
just the embers of a fire nearby,

still smouldering, a pair of jeans, some tee
shirts dripping on a branch from last

night's rain, a sullen bird of paradise
what else? picking at a half-chewed fruit.

Lorna Thorpe

LOWER MARKET STREET, 1973

Bombed on Tuinal and Newcastle Brown,
Mad Eddie steams into our room, skids
to a halt at our bed and throws back the sheet,
squealing, 'Ah, look at the babes in the wood'.
Naked as eels, me and Richard cling to each other.
But I drop acid, I'm on the Pill. I want to be as cool
as hennaed Sadie, who's crashing on our floor,
pops Mogadon for breakfast and bares
her boyish tits without thinking, who'll steal
my green platform boots when she leaves.
Grabbing his balls, Eddie flickers his tongue
across his teeth, looking at me like he knows
about the boys I've let feel me up in alleys,
that I lost my virginity to a policeman's son
in Stanmer Park. Richard tells me I'm all woman,
I try on the tag but here come breasts, hair, blood,
here comes the creature my father couldn't have
in the house, the one who was only loveable
when she was a baby, a disc of pink vinyl,
stamped with her master's voice.

Jane Weir

On the Recommendation of Ovid We Tried a Weasel

It was the first mammal he ever gave me.
He must have trapped it late last night when the moon
disappeared inside a nightclub of clouds
and stars giggling staggered behind.

I found it in the morning, slung like an amulet
across the lapel of my winter coat, flattened to a strip,
satin lined, its snout firm like the tip of a snooker cue,
black tipped and bloody.

In truth he'd tried other things, such as the skins of a dozen
pulverized rattle snakes, the milk from a score
of white iced rabbits, a pot of crayfish.

Then there were the showers of flowers.
Oh yes, the flowers, barrow boy loads of flowers,
such as the biblical *Selaginella*,
a cruciferous plant that he said –
if I ever reached full term – was believed
as it bloomed to smooth out the suffering of delivery.

He was known to serenade me in my sleep
with those hollowed out Halloween
gourds favoured by percussionists;
for it's said the loose pieces left inside
simulate the rattling sound of an embryo.

What else can I say – we tried and tried.
I practically wore the weasel to death.
Ask yourself, how many times can you scrape
the bottom of a barrel? He shocked me with a rat,
a dead cat dredged from a sacred river bed.
I drew the line. He gave up after that.

I'm Trying to Make Gnocchi di Patate for Angelina for Old Times Sake

When the potato puree's dry
enough I add flour, butter, eggs,
season well, knead to a dough.
One thing I forgot to say –
many times I had to
brush your bronzed hands away,
as you tried to play
scales over me.
No different from that day
we found those shadows
lounging in the dusky
corner of a fifteenth century chapel,
and slim your fingers picked
and unpicked like an inquisition
at the hook and eye
of my bra strap,
until it broke free, flew
askew like a bat and my breasts
soared from the cartilage
curves of its satin uplift…
I banished you with the civet
to the other end of the island.
From afar I let you gaze towards a star,
as I roll and cut small cylinders,
that in turn become dimpled crescents,
like the spores underneath
an up-turned leaf.
I drop each crescent one by one,
whilst grinning, you heat the plate.
Both of us are drinking Chianti.
It takes about three minutes.
I know because I've learned to gauge –
like all good cooks do.
I serve it simple,

in the Genoese way –
with pesto.
Flushed, a loose strand
or two straying,
I sit across the table
and pass you the fork,
the swooning plate.
For your Mothers sake
stop looking at me
that way – start eating.

Arnold Wesker

She Waits, He Hesitates

She waits, he hesitates
He has the fear of male
She the female's certitude.

Where he comes from she went.
What he abandoned she adored.

Adoring, he hesitates
Why she waits he cannot fathom.
She is familiar with such men.
Familiar, she waits.

In between the waiting hesitating play
Is silence. His uncertainty
Her contempt, spread like calm
Before the storm.

'Form is all.' Finally she broke
The Carthusian pact.
'All is known
Predictable, banal.'

'If all is form, what,' he asked,
'Is there in you for me to hold?'
He waits. She hesitates.

Between the waiting hesitating play
Sides change. The certitude
Is his. The fear hers.

Jackie Wills

Love Song for Fidel Castro

They've started a tight salsa
when Elisa strolls on, hips round as a drum.

Her band whoops, edges up the percussion
and the bass whips her calves.

She looks at each woman, remembering
how she brought them together,

their babies now workers, mothers,
or fathers, grins at the years they display

in their breasts, waists and eyes,
one thousand, three hundred and three.

She nods to Aleida on congas holding rivers
in her palms and Mathilda, the oldest,

on rhythm guitar, playing just as she's waited
in a chair by the door, night after night all her life.

Elisa turns to the room, finds the President's table,
puts a mike to her mouth.

'For this man tonight, twenty lovers,' she jokes
and her eyes won't leave as she sings

of sun in the citrus, Batista,
all the sweat and fists in the wind,

of a child in a cellar, paths through the cane,
the wings on every island's shoulder blades.

She sings of the speeches scrolled in his pockets,
of Angola, Mandela, his friend.

She sings of Havana, how it still burns
on maps of the world,

of Martí's white rose and an exile's return
to the Island of Youth.

Then she picks up the claves and the crowd
shines the floor with its footwork,

as they dance the way heat breaks
the line of a road, each beat and bell of the salsa,

a gasp in the hand.

Samantha Wynne-Rhydderch

CRAYFISH TAIL SALSA

Hotel Reception

8 stone 2.
There's only so far you can go
on an island a mile long.
That was just on Wednesdays,
my day off. On the other six
I'd spend eight hours a day in a
cupboard. True, every office has one
you can escape to. There,
it *was* the office,
a sixteenth-century one at that.
I'd hear reports, of course,
from the world outside the castle walls.
What did I see of it? Sixty seconds
of sunset when I'd run outside
to change the daily menus,
a new version of the same poem.

Kitchen

8 stone.
On a good day and if he hadn't had
that extra pint at lunchtime,
the head chef, Jim, would only
scream at me twice to f— off
when I'd go in at five to get
the menu checked. Ravenous
as I was, there was no place
I'd rather not be than hear the reply to
Any changes to the menu, Jim?
Crayfish Tail Salsa was one
his glass eye would miss,

that little dance in sauce tripping
off the page. The closest I came
all year to writing poems was
deciding where the line breaks would go
in the menus Jim would spit out.
By the way what's the difference
between 'a tossed salad' and 'a salad'?
Isn't all salad tossed? By a tosser?

Hunger

7 stone 12.
Working in a hotel? F**r St*r food every day!
Chips mainly. *Look at this*
one of the kitchen girls hissed
opening a fist to reveal the dull eye
of a fish. Any good at problem solving?
If staff tea is at 5 every day
and you are on duty 2 till 10pm
six days with no breaks,
how do you eat? Leave your desk
for one minute, whisk out a side plate
containing four mouthfuls
of cold mushroom risotto. Feast
on the dishes of the menu as you
type them out. Read the checks
slowly: 2 x camembert,
2 x pheasant, 1 x mousse.
At 10 I'd be allowed to
pick fruit out of the bin
whilst a waiter soothed the floor
with water, shoulderblade to the wall,
Woody Guthrie throating out cotton field lyric
long forty years ago.

Anger

7 stone 3.
A juggler of irons and phones, cream teas
and keys. Not that he'd see it that way,
your boss. The best way to run a hotel is
to get one person to do three jobs. PS. It's you.
Why not write a one-act play
in your head while answering two phones?
Scene 1 is where you're limping
with an iron and board to room 42,
sprinting back in Manolos
to make tea for six in the library
whilst a colonel is waiting
to be shown to the conservatory.
In Scene 2 you're already
answering line 1 when line 2 rings.
Why don't you answer the phone!

There's a lady at the poolside
who wants fresh towels! With jam?
It would be funny if it wasn't
happening to me, six days a week
for a year. I didn't bother writing Scene 3.

Dungeon

7 stone.
After dinner, they'd all repair to the Dungeon Bar,
the guests, the chefs and the chambermaids,
freshly pressed after Turndown.
It would be as if the rooms had been visited by a
fairy who riffled through the linen and folded open
the first page of the Book of Bed.
Sleep on this, the sheets seemed to speak,
these beds of weddings: the low-key,
the high-powered, the third time around.

Occasionally I'd drink there too, in the bar,
celebrating the arrivals and departures
of those who'd been to a cinema only two nights before.

Leaving the Island

6 stone 13.
Flowers. That's what kept you going all year,
wasn't it? A bunch of sweet peas
I'd buy for a pound once a week,
their smell so delicious I could've
eaten them. Except by then I'd lost
my appetite. Three days to go, said
the calendar. I was too weak to
carry my case down to the quay,
so they drove me those a hundred yards
in a boneshaker Land-Rover.
Every flight and ferry cancelled by storms,
there was only one way out.
I caught the freight ship back
to England in a thirty-five-knot wind.
So that was me and four crewmen for five hours
in heavy seas. I queased
on deck watching it all recede:
the parapets, the gardens, the boathouse,
the agapanthas, Watermill Cove where
something had eluded me at the water's edge
in the sharp light of autumn, birdcall purpling
away. When I could fit it all into
the palm of my hand, I held my hunger
there like the one pebble I brought back
as a souvenir. At the dockside
in Penzance I floated off the ship and did a
little jig. *What's that?* they said. *Crayfish
Tail Salsa, that little dance in sauce I never got
to taste*, I said and headed off to
the poshest restaurant in town.

Publisher acknowledgements

Patience Agbabi · EAT ME · *Bloodshot Monochrome* · Canongate

Moniza Alvi · THE CROSSING · *Europa* · Bloodaxe Books

Simon Armitage · *from* OUT OF THE BLUE · *Out of the Blue* · Enitharmon Press

Annemarie Austin · AVOIDED SUBJECT · *Very* · Bloodaxe Books

Simon Barraclough · FUSING THE BRAIDS · LONDON WHALE · *Los Alamos Mon Amour* · Salt Publishing

Bob Beagrie · THE LINESMAN · *Yoik* · Cinnamon Press

Sujata Bhatt · WHAT IS EXOTIC? · A HOUSE OF SILENCE · *Pure Lizard* · Carcanet Press

Pat Borthwick · THE WIDOWER'S BUTTON · Envoi Poetry Competition

Sue Boyle · A LEISURE CENTRE IS ALSO A TEMPLE OF LEARNING · *The Rialto*

Lawrence Bradby · THE PORT · Smiths Knoll

Colette Bryce · THE KNACK · *Self-Portrait in the Dark* · Picador

Christopher Buehlman · WANTON · The Bridport Prize

John Burnside · AN ESSAY CONCERNING SOLITUDE · *Poetry Review*

Stephen Burt · PEONIES · *London Review of Books*

Ciaran Carson · L'AIR DU TEMPS · *For All We Know* · Gallery Books

Angela Cleland · PEELING · *And in here, the Menagerie* · Templar Poetry

Robert Crawford · FULL VOLUME · *Full Volume* · Jonathan Cape

Bernadette Cremin · NADIA · *Speechless* · Waterloo Press

J P Dancing Bear · NATURAL ENEMIES · *Conflicted Light* · Salmon Poetry

Isobel Dixon · MEET MY FATHER · *A Fold in the Map* · Salt Publishing

Maura Dooley · THE FINAL STAGES OF DIPLOMACY · *Life Under Water* · Bloodaxe Books

Stephen Dunn · REPLICAS · *Everything Else in the World* · W W Norton & Company

Mark Ford · SIGNS OF THE TIMES · *London Review of Books*

Andrew Forster · CHOOSING TO DISAPPEAR · THE HORSES · *Fear of Thunder* · Flambard Press

Adam Foulds · 5: NIGHT FIRES · *The Broken Word* · Jonathan Cape

John Fuller · MY LIFE ON THE MARGINS OF CELEBRITY · *Song & Dance* · Chatto & Windus

Sam Gardiner · BRAVE FACE · Dream Catcher

Deborah Garrison · I SAW YOU WALKING · *The Second Child* · Bloodaxe Books

Lavinia Greenlaw · WINTER FINDING · *Poetry Review*

Jane Griffiths · TERRITORIAL · THE PRINTER · *Another Country* · Bloodaxe Books

Paul Groves · AGAINST STEREOTYPE · *Qwerty* · Seren

Kelly Grovier · CAMPING OUT · *A Lens in the Palm* · Oxford Poets (Carcanet Press)

Jen Hadfield · CANIS MINOR · ODYSSEUS AND THE SOU'WESTER · *Nigh-No-Place* · Bloodaxe Books

Seamus Heaney · CUTAWAYS · *Irish Pages*

Paul Henry · THE BLACK GUITAR · *Ingrid's Husband* · Seren

Kevin Higgins · MY MILITANT TENDENCY · *Time Gentlemen, Please* · Salmon Poetry

Peter Howard · THE USES OF MOWN GRASS · *Weighing the Air* · Arrowhead Press

Mick Imlah · INKHORN · THE AYRSHIRE OPHEUS · *The Lost Leader* · Faber and Faber

Katia Kapovich · THE GIRL THAT SAVED A VILLAGE · *Cossacks and Bandits* · Salt Publishing

Mimi Khalvati · IMPENDING WHITENESS · Acumen

John Kinsella · COLOURS OF THE WHEATBELT · *Shades of the Sublime & Beautiful* · Picador

Frances Leviston · DRAGONFLIES · LAMPADROME · *Public Dream* · Picador

James Liddy · AN EXCURSION WITH IAN GIBSON TO THE LORCA MUSEUM · *The Shop*

Jamie McKendrick · THE KEY · AN ENCROACHMENT · *Crocodiles & Obelisks* · Faber and Faber

Anna McKerrow · OCCASIONAL LOVER · *The Fast Heat of Beauty* · Flambard Press

Allison McVety · HOW YOU CAN KNOW A PLACE · BOY ON THE BUS · *The Night Trotsky Came to Stay* · Smith/Doorstop Books

Richard Marggraf Turley · ANNING · *The Fossil-Box* · Cinnamon Press

Valeria Melchioretto · THE TEAR PERCOLATOR · *The End of Limbo* · Salt Publishing

Matt Merritt · HOLIDAY, 1939 · *Troy Town* · Arrowhead Press

David Morley · BEARS · *The Invisible Kings* · Carcanet Press

Stephanie Norgate · BIRTH · THE PHONE TOWER WOOD · *Hidden River* · Bloodaxe Books

Julie O'Callaghan · LETTERGESH STRAND · *Tell Me This is Normal* · Bloodaxe Books

Ciaran O'Driscoll · PLEASE HOLD · Southword Editions

Catherine Ormell · CAMPAIGN DESK, DECEMBER 1812 · The Bridport Prize

Niall O'Sullivan · THE FATHER IN LAW · *Ventriloquism for Monkeys* · Waterways

Alice Oswald · TWO MOON POEMS · *Poetry Review*

Don Paterson · LOVE POEM FOR NATALIE 'TUSJA' BERIDZE · *Poetry Review*

Victoria Pugh · ALL THAT GLISTERS · *Mrs Marvellous* · Two Rivers Press

Angela Readman · HOUSEWIFE · *Strip* · Salt Publishing

Robin Robertson · BY CLACHAN BRIDGE · *London Review of Books*

Kate Rhodes · WELLS-NEXT-THE-SEA · The Bridport Prize

Stephen Romer · MAGISTRATE · *Yellow Studio* · Oxford Poets (Carcanet Press)

Carol Rumens · CLOTHES LEFT ON A WASHING-LINE · *Blind Spots* · Seren

Lorna Shaughnessy · GRASPING THE NETTLE · *Torching the Brown River* · Salmon Poetry

Kathryn Simmonds · THE BOYS IN THE FISH SHOP · HANDBAG THIEF · *Sunday at the Skin Launderette* · Seren

Catherine Smith · SNAKEBITE · PICNIC · *Lip* · Smith/Doorstop Books

Jean Sprackland · MATTRESSES · *Tilt* · Jonathan Cape

Greta Stoddart · WANT · *Salvation Jane* · Anvil Press Poetry

Maggie Sullivan · AN EVERYDAY EPIC · *near death (domestic)* · tall-lighthouse

Michael Symmons Roberts · ORIGIN OF SPECIES · *The Half Healed* · Jonathan Cape

Lorna Thorpe · LOWER MARKET STREET, 1973 · *A Ghost in My House* · Arc Publications

Tim Turnbull · ODE ON A GRAYSON PERRY URN · *Magma Poetry*

Jane Weir · ON THE RECOMMENDATION OF OVID WE TRIED A WEASEL · Wigtown Poetry Competition

Jane Weir · I'm Trying to Make Gnocchi di Patate for Angelina for Old Times Sake · *Before Playing Romeo* · Templar Poetry

Arnold Wesker · She Waits, He Hesitates · *All Things Tire of Themselves* · Flambard Press

Jackie Wills · Love Song for Fidel Castro · *Commandments* · Arc Publications

Samantha Wynne-Rhydderch · Crayfish Tail Salsa · *Not in These Shoes* · Picador